The Power of Paper

How to Create Wealth by Investing in Mortgages

Written by
Troy Fullwood

Copyright © 2018 Troy Fullwood

Published by Branded Expert Publishing

ISBN-13:978-1987482485

ISBN-10:1987482484

Legal Description

All Rights Reserved. No part of this publication may be reproduced in any form or by any means, including scanning, photocopying, or otherwise without prior written permission of the copyright holder.

Disclaimer and Terms of Use: The Author and Publisher have strived to be as accurate and complete as possible in the creation of this book, notwithstanding the fact that they do not warrant or represent at any time that the contents within are accurate due to the rapidly changing nature of the business. While all attempts have been made to verify information provided in this publication, the Author and Publisher assume no responsibility for errors, omissions, or contrary interpretation of the subject matter herein. Any perceived slights of specific persons, peoples, or organizations are unintentional. In practical advice books, like anything else in life, there are no guarantees of income made. Readers are cautioned to rely on their own judgment about their individual circumstances to act accordingly. This book is not intended for use as a source of legal, business, accounting, real estate or financial advice. All readers are advised to seek services of competent professionals in the legal, business, accounting, real estate and finance fields.

Dedication

I dedicate this book to my wonderful wife, Kim and 5 amazing children: Lauren, Hunter, Jack, Camden and Parker.

Thank you for all of your love and support as I have followed my dreams to educate and support people who are passionate about achieving their financial goals.

Every day I give thanks to God, for blessing me with all of you.

Table of Contents

Introduction vii

Chapter 1: 1
Turning Dirt into Diamonds

Chapter 2: 11
How to Find Notes

Chapter 3: 25
Due Diligence

Chapter 4: 41
Servicing and Creating a Better Product

Chapter 5: 49
Servicing in Today's Era

Chapter 6: 61
Yields and Returns on Capital

Chapter 7: 73
Passive Investors

Chapter 8: 81
Time Value of Money

Chapter 9: 97
Property Titles

Chapter 10: 105
Performing Notes – Wholesaling vs Investor

Conclusion 119

Free Investor Resources 123

About the Author 125

The Power of Paper

Introduction

"Compound interest is the eighth wonder of the world. He who understands it, earns it ... he who doesn't ... pays it."
~ Albert Einstein ~

I don't consider myself in the paper business. I'm in the solving financial problems for people business. I just happen to use paper as a vehicle.

There are more varieties of notes today and people are starting to use them in different ways

Can you relate to this scenario? I had a very sweet lady who inherited some notes from her husband when he died. She found herself being a paper manager when she had no idea what paper was. She was clueless. She told me, "I have no idea what to even do with this stuff." I sat down with her, went over everything, and as we outlined a plan, she told me that all she really wanted to do was travel. She wanted to go see her grandkids more and go spend time with her daughter who lived several states away. This veered me in the right direction. She was able to sell her home and move closer to her family. She was very grateful and told me, "This is what I've always wanted." I was able to make her dream come true, while also preserving her husband's efforts and his desire to look out for her.

Good information is imperative to people's success. I see that there are a lot of people involved in real estate nowadays, especially the fix and flip market. I see the banks are not addressing the underserved side of the consumer base, meaning people that earn less than $150,000. Home ownership, as far as home values go, is not typically served or addressed by the banks. There's this higher percentage of our population that ultimately, for lack of better words, is shooting from the hip in trying to do the right thing. Their goal is to do the right thing, but they keep missing the target. Ultimately, when they miss the target, it costs them money. That money can add up to tens of thousands of dollars.

The industry as a whole has started to learn about paper, but they really don't understand how to fine-tune what they're doing. It's kind of like the idea of writing a book. We can go to the library and see all kinds of books all day long, but how does it get from our head to the paper? The same thing is true in the note and paper business as a whole. You'd be surprised how fragmented it really is.

My mission is to help people that are in the residential real estate investing market, but they're wandering around, trying to figure out what they would like to do. These are typically people that are jumping from seminar to seminar, looking to figure out what they want to do.

The goal of writing this book is to create a resource manual for investors who are using this model and this technique in their business to grow their business. To help them produce better quality notes. To help them get more money out of their notes when they sell them. It's not necessarily tied to higher interest rates or shorter terms, it's tied to a variety of things. I'm going to get into more of that as the book goes on.

The more people that have a copy of this book, the better they're going to be as investors. I'm in Arizona, but even in Arizona I haven't talked to all the folks here. This puts that word out there and helps people to have a manuscript/game plan for helping more and more people all the time. I feel that It's an underserved market.

I think there's a lot of people out there that have the desire. They want to do better, they want to create better loans. They want to create better deals, and hopefully this helps them accomplish that.

The Power of Paper

I learned years ago that if you can solve problems, you can make very good money doing it. There's always going to be problems and there's always going to be a need and there's always going to be a reason for it. I enjoy what I do, working with notes, because it brings about different challenges all the time.

I want this to be the beginning of a relationship with me, my office and the readers of our book, not the end.

Going forward I will be covering all different kinds of paper, but in the end, I want to show you what kind of paper actually works best.

Troy Fullwood

The Power of Paper

The Power of Paper

Chapter 1

How I Turned Dirt into Real Estate Notes

I've always been an entrepreneur. When I graduated from high school, I was already running a successful landscaping firm. I found myself going to college part-time, taking business management courses. My freshman year, I found myself at odds with one of my professors who didn't like a paper that I had written about a business. I was actually referring to my landscaping business and he felt that my paper was not textbook. He was looking for a "textbook type" case. Mind you, this was back around 1985. Unfortunately for that time period they really didn't understand case studies. They taught from the book and that was it. It was the professor's way or no way.

Ultimately, we agreed to disagree on the subject matter about earning a person's business. I used the case study from a municipality job that I had been on. As I went through it he felt like it was very inconsistent to the message that he was teaching to the class. After that, I saw very quickly that his eyes were not looking at the same thing that my eyes were looking at. I dropped out of college and went back home to my mom and my dad and said, "You know guys, go ahead and keep the money that you had set aside for me and give it to my little sister. I'm going to go on and keep running my landscaping business." It was in that moment that I realized that in my goal of becoming a multi-millionaire, I was trying to learn how to become a millionaire from somebody who was making $60,000 a year as a professor, and that's not how it works!

By professor standards that was good money and he was very successful as a professor, but he was never going to be successful as a business entrepreneur. I was more excited about becoming a successful entrepreneur than I was being a college student or getting a college degree. I was fortunate enough that the clients in my life were all

The Power of Paper

business owners. When you're running a landscape/lawn mowing service, you learn that it's a luxury item and people that can afford that service are typically successful people, in the entrepreneurial realm. I was constantly being mentored by my clients in a lot of different ways. It was really something that I cherish to this day.

I went on to grow that company and ultimately sold it. I was then contacted by a chemical fertilization company to work for them. While there, I was able to grow their commercial division. I guess I was noticed, because the next thing I know I'm being hired by a very well-known PGA pro golfer, Ben Crenshaw, to run his turf grass management business. Under his guidance, I grew and learned a lot more about high level business.

It was during this time that I stumbled across an attorney who was in the business of buying performing first lien notes. Not only did he buy them, he helped his investors close them. He had a master portfolio worth around $4 million under his own guidance. He started teaching me the nuances and the art of seller financing. He took me under his wing and taught me everything he could about the overall business. He taught me about helping people obtain home ownership, where they otherwise wouldn't have the possibility to do so. With that knowledge, I went on a journey, building a business around that model. That was 21 life-changing years ago.

Early on in my journey I ran into a friend of a friend. He had accumulated over 700 real estate notes that he had on homes that he had bought and seller financed. He, too, took me under his wings. I ultimately helped him liquidate some of his portfolio so he could cash out some of his investors. With that I learned the art of organization and the importance of due diligence in that space. He ultimately liquidated about 50 loans from this portfolio over a six-month period and because lack of organization, it taught me the business of fixing, repairing, correcting and ultimately building a file that had value to it. That was the start of a 21-year journey of taking what I'd learned from both of my mentors, applying it and building a model around it, when there was no model in the industry.

There was nothing 21 years ago. Facebook wasn't around, the internet wasn't as user friendly as it is today, and Google didn't exist. There weren't many tools or resources we could use in the industry. Just a lot of snail mail, FedEx and people down at the court house working for us.

We did it all by hand; newspapers, classified ads and courthouse document review. All of those things that people turn their nose up nowadays because it's so user friendly from the comfort of a laptop. Although I don't typically do those things anymore, it really gave me a huge respect for what I would call the "old timers" or pioneers of the industry.

The industry's become more institutionalized. Now there's more banks involved. At one point, the Ford Motor Corporation was involved, as well as a number of other big, well-known companies. Some of them are still around, some of them have journeyed or ventured into other industries and have set this aside. The point being that the business and the industry today is so much bigger than what it used to be. It's very user friendly in today's marketplace. That's something that is exciting because of the speed in which people can take action.

My passion behind getting involved in the business was that I really wanted to be a part of an industry that had a major impact on people's lives. I didn't really want to do the fix and flip or the brick and mortar rental properties because it really didn't fit who I was and the goals I wanted to achieve in my business.

Let me state that I have a tremendous amount of respect for the people that do that because they add so much value to the communities and neighborhoods nationwide. When they do go out there and fix up homes and provide that opportunity for home ownership, we found that we can come alongside those folks and ultimately help them grow their business. By adding a financial arm to their business model in the form of seller financing, in helping them to assemble that loan or note. It's sellable to the marketplace. Often, people forget that what they're creating needs to be sellable. Just because you have a note and a mortgage on a property doesn't necessarily constitute something that's sellable. Especially now, in today's era of Dodd Frank, where there are guidelines that have to be followed.

One of those key guidelines is the ability to repay the loan. We add a value service to them by sharing with them actual tools and resources that ultimately help them do that correctly and effectively so that they are putting together high-quality loans to ultimately sell. For instance, if a wealth investor were to rehab a home or fix up a home, they would not paint that home bright pink because the industry tells them, "Don't do this bright pink because nobody will buy a bright pink house. If you paint it earth tone or neutral colors, then your success rate in selling that property is going to increase exponentially."

The same thing is true with real estate notes as a whole. You want to make sure you've got key elements so that it's sellable and somebody truly wants to buy it. Otherwise, you could find yourself holding on to that note for a longer period of time than you've anticipated.

Learning the Hard Way

When I got started in the business and learning from my attorney friend, after about five days he patted me on the back and said, "You know, go get 'em tiger." I went back home and started scratching my head because there was no marketing strategy or plan. It was just like, "There you go. Good luck." As I started trying to piece it all together, I had this

The Power of Paper

idea to put an ad in the San Antonio Express newspaper, which is where I lived. It was about three lines, with my phone number, and it said, "Top dollar paid for notes and mortgages. Call." I put the ad in on a Monday and found out on a Tuesday that I had to go in for out-patient surgery on Friday.

I showed up at the hospital, had my hernia surgery, they gave me a bunch of pain meds, and I went home and laid on the couch. I'd listed my home phone number because I didn't have an office number. People started calling off the ad and answered and started just talking. People often ask me what I said and to this day I have no idea what I said! I guess the pain pills worked. Well, a lady showed up at my door with a file full of paperwork on Saturday morning. My roommate opened the door and she said, "I'm here to talk to Troy." I was horizontal on the couch because I couldn't move.

She saw me laying on the couch and handed the paperwork to my roommate. I told her that I would look it over that weekend and get back with her. I ended up getting back with her Monday and on Tuesday got the deal under contract. It was something that her husband actually created when he sold one of his fix and flip properties. They were looking to cash out on the note to do another house.

That was the first deal I ever did as a broker and I brokered the deal to the Associates Financial Services. They gave me a price and I took my fee out of the deal.

Wish I could remember what I told her over the phone that day!

My next deal was on a house in Lotus, Texas. It was a little $35,000 note where they had put down less than 5%. It was a big trend back then when people were putting minimums downs. The interest rate on their loan was 14%.

The Power of Paper

This particular couple, married with two children, went out and refinanced the loan at a local bank in the area. It was very common with those small-town communities where there's always one or two local banks that would finance those smaller balanced loans. They lowered their interest rate down to about 7%, which put more money in their pocket and obviously paid off their loan in a shorter period of time.

This may sound like it was a bad thing for me because I wasn't getting 14% interest, but I like loans that have that no prepayment penalty. On the plus side, they would come in and pay this off sooner, which means that that interest that I yield on that loan actually skyrockets. In that particular case, it was 14% for 30 years. When they paid off the loan, which was two and a half years later, our interest rate was running around 32% yield on that particular deal.

When we bought it, the face rate of the loan was 14%. We bought it at 70% UPB, which put the yield on that particular deal. We came in and bought this at a 22% yield. When they sold it, it jumped up to 33%. The reason it did that was because we no longer have that term that goes out 30 years. We now have condensed it down to two and a half years, but we still bought it at the yield, which meant that we got that spread. We earned that back sooner versus later. In other words, it coincided with the time value of money.

I want to stress to people that I have a 14% interest rate face amount, or that's written into the note of the mortgage. I didn't give the seller of that note the full value. I only gave him $24,000 for that note, and that's what raised the yield to 22%, spread over 30 years. When they shortened up the period, it actually raised my yield because of the original discount.

It's interesting, because at the beginning of my career in this industry, it was very common place that notes were created with interest rates anywhere from 12% to the highest I ever saw 23%. In some states, like Arizona and Texas, there's no usury law.

It's interesting when you compare the industry 21 years ago to the industry today. How much it's evolved, but also, what used to be standard then is "out of this world" type ideas. What's standard today is something of a whole different matter. Meaning that people become much more educated and much more in-tune financially, which is wonderful. You don't see people buying houses with 14% interest anymore. Even what I call the subprime market, people think that's always been a 4% or 5% market. Actually, subprime used to be 12% money, even from the banks.

Why Sell a Note?

People always wonder why someone would sell their notes at a discount. One of the reasons is having a purpose you can use the money for where you'll make even more than what you were making on the note.

It's a very popular reason for investors. They create a lot of notes and they sell them because their model and their team is built on fixing and repairing and selling houses, not carrying back paper. They do that because they have a buyer who can't qualify through traditional means (banks or institutions). The bank has the luxury of picking and choosing who they want to lend money to. They pick and choose based on a person's financial ability and whether or not they can qualify for what's typically known as full doc loans.

Up to 80% of the general public can't qualify for a bank loan. Maybe they just started a new job, or a new career, or they just graduated college or they're self-employed and haven't filed their taxes for a couple of years. There's a lot of different 'real world' aspects to everybody's life. The banks understand that but they don't really care about that. They want to know 'can you fit in our box, and if you can we'd love to do business with you. If you can't, we're sorry.' They leave people to fend for themselves.

The beauty of the internet is that people have educated themselves on other options. Rent to own, leasing, lease purchases, etc. They've also learned that they can buy homes with seller financing and they'll go and look for those types of properties to purchase. That's the beauty of it because I think the people that are offering that offer a very valuable service for people seeking out home ownership for the first time. Although I think the banks have gotten better, I think they still have a long way to go. I think that the free market has a tendency to dictate the direction that people are going to move towards. In other words, people aren't going to sit around waiting for the banks to come up with a perfect loan for them. They're going to go do what they have to do to provide for their family and to succeed on their own.

It's such an amazing industry because there are some boundaries and there are golden rules everybody needs to follow. Outside of that, there really is nothing. In other words, if I'm sitting down with you and we're negotiating on the purchase of a home, whatever we do creates a win-win relationship for both. However, there are some basic things that you need to be sure of. You want to make sure people put down payments of ideally around 10%. You want to make sure they have decent credit and that they have a job. You want to make sure that the deal is something that's healthy for both parties, meaning 10, 20, 30- year terms at reasonable rates, at a 6% to 9% interest rate.

Currently that is the market exactly. The beautiful thing about that is, it gives people that home ownership opportunity. It also helps that seller sell more homes. That money goes back into their portfolio for the next project or the next property. Ultimately, that money then goes back into the economy. When you see that happening all over the country, in every city within the country, it shows me that people are really driven towards being part of the solution. In these communities and neighborhoods in cities around the country where banks are not serving, it's an underserved part of our nation. This gives those people that opportunity to be a homeowner and to raise their family in neighborhoods that they want to be in. Go to schools where they can get an education and go the church of their choice and things of that nature.

To me it's a plus. It's a very positive thing and it's not always about high interest rates. It's all about being a starting point. The beautiful thing about that is it can change and grow over time as people and families and communities change and grow as well.

The Power of Paper

Chapter 2

How to Find Notes

Ove the years I've been asked, "Troy, I've got some money and I'm interested in investing. How do I find one of these notes?"

There's a couple of things that people need to understand about buying notes, and part of it has to do with the marketing side of it and part of it has to do with the research and discovery side of it.

When we're looking for notes and we're speaking about single family residential performing first lien notes, in this particular case, we're looking for things that would be marketed in the open marketplace on a nationwide basis here in the U.S. They would be marketed as owner will carry, owner financing, owner carry back, seller carry back, seller financing and seller will carry.

This may shock you, but one of the best places to find real estate notes is through an evergreen marketing system, like Craigslist. Craigslist is that overlooked portal that people tend to forget because it's not nouveau anymore, it's been around for a long time and people know it's there, they use it, but they don't really use it to its potential.

So, what we've learned over the years is that when we're looking to deploy capital in the space, and if we have a lull in our business, or even when we're showing people how to get started, we point them directly to Craigslist. There's a good reason for that. People are constantly listing properties for sale, both residential and commercial. The words that I just shared with you, "the seller will carry" and "owner financing" are key words that they're using to market their properties. These are people that are ready to sell their property. They are looking for buyers and they are looking for people to purchase the home and then ultimately, they're going to sell the note.

Now the beautiful thing about that is that there are two ways to look at this. One is when you work with these people on the front side you can help them structure deals exactly to your liking, so it gives you that insight to guide them to put together a note that you can purchase and put in your portfolio that performs and creates the returns that you're looking for. Most of the time, when people don't have that guidance, they put their best foot forward, but they will leave out key details like they will do a low interest rate, or they will do a low-down payment where they forget to check the borrower's credit, or they put extended terms on the loan, or they do interest only. And a lot of those types of details are what affect the overall quality of the paper, or the note, that they're creating. So that's a great place to look, not to mention that it's kind of a revolving door in the sense that the properties fall off at about the 45-day mark, so you've got new fresh opportunities coming to you on a daily/weekly basis, depending upon how aggressive you are in buying product.

I want to mention, too, that these tend to be direct seller contacts rather than going through an agent, which is much, much easier to work with if you can get that third party out of the way and directly deal with who's going to be the note owner. A crucial detail in creating success in a transaction is if you can talk directly to the note holder or note seller. You're going to get a much clearer message about the overall quality of the property and the overall quality of the paper or note that they're creating, and so you are going to get firsthand information versus having it go through a chain of people.

Now, the best place to find these on Craigslist is simply by going to the real estate section in your city of choice, clicking on "Real Estate" and then going up to the search bar and just typing in the key words that I shared with you a little bit ago, owner finance, owner will carry. Every city has a tendency to favor one type of terminology over another. The only insight that I have for that is the difference between the way that they say it. Example, in New York they say pie, in Arizona we say pizza. So, it really has to do with the area of the country that people live in and how they associate the word language and use it, but that's why I gave you a plethora of opportunities to use different word phrases, because that will bring up different amounts of opportunities in that area. Therefore, Craigslist is number one because it's evergreen.

Another place you can go is to our website,

http://mortgageinvestorpro.com/resource/,

which has a list of investor clubs nationwide.

A third place to look would be with local realtors who deal in and represent sellers who are selling properties with owner financing. Now, what you typically find in that space is that most realtors are going to go with what I call their Plan A, which is to take on the listing, list it under normal channels like the MLS and various other realtor websites, and once they spend a certain period of time with that property, say six months or greater, they will start looking at other opportunities and other methods on how to sell that property and they'll turn their attention to doing seller financing or offering owner will carry for their seller. And obviously the same rules apply as far as down payment, credit worthiness, things of that nature, but they are a great source for deals that I would label more as a long-term listing, something that they've had on their books for an extended period of time.

A fourth place to look would be the servicing division of local title companies. The large title companies that we know on a nationwide basis, places like First American, Fidelity Title, Stewart Title, Chicago

The Power of Paper

Title, Lawyers Title, all of those title companies have a servicing division within their organization and they're typically on a state-wide basis. Case in point: First American Title here in Phoenix, Arizona has their servicing division located on Washington Street, on the outskirts of downtown Phoenix. That also happens to be their main processing center for the state of Arizona.

Each state has a division, and sometimes have multiple locations in states if they're larger, like Texas, California and Florida. The purpose in doing that is because someone will carry back a note on the properties that they've sold, they'll close the transaction in the title company and the title company will offer up their services to collect the payments and post them and issue year end interest statements for the note holder. Ultimately, over a period of time, we find once that note gets to a nine to fifteen-month range, the note holder no longer has any interest in continuing to collect payments. They'd much rather have a lump sum of cash versus the five or six or eight hundred dollars a month payment that they're currently collecting. They find that their life has maybe changed a little bit. They see where they could put that lump sum of money into a different investment, into a different opportunity and now they are looking to sell it. So, having those relationships with those servicing divisions is an important part of getting deal flow and opportunity to come to you.

Now a little secret... if you offer to pick up the postage for the servicing division for a certain percentage of the monthly statements that they send out to the note holders, which basically means that they've collected the payment, they're issuing the checks, they're sending out a monthly statement to the note holder, they'll do a drop insert. You have to pay for the drop insert, you have to have it designed and printed, but they'll put that drop insert in there if you pick up the postage fee for the cost of "X" number of mailings. Let's say you want to pay for 2,000 of these mailings, so you'll pay the postage on 2,000 of those to go out. They typically want three to six-month commitment, but you're putting your advertising in with that note holder's statement and that note holder's check. You can include a message to them that connects with them in a way where they would take action and contact you as a note buyer to purchase that particular deal.

So that's one way of opening the door that speaks volumes to servicing companies. They can cut down on their costs because you are picking up that cost and ultimately you pick up deals as well, so it's a very direct marketing source. Not to mention, when a place like First American or Lawyers Title or Fidelity Title puts that inside of a statement they're endorsing your company, they're endorsing your business, and they're endorsing you as a note buyer. That speaks volumes on a referral type basis for them.

The other thing that you could do is you can also offer to them a note holder's handbook which you can download by going to http://www.pinnacle-investments.com. The note holder's handbook will allow you to catch the note holders on the front side at the title company when they're closing the deal. You can actually brand the note holder's handbook with your information and the title company's information by simply using somebody like Kinko's. You can create a dozen or so handbooks, take them to the escrow department at the title company and as they close deals that have seller financing, kindly ask them to hand out the note holder's handbook to their client, which has all of your contact information as well as theirs. It's a great book, it's a great resource, feel free to download it at this site, http://www.pinnacle-investments.com.

The next thing is real estate attorneys. Real estate attorneys often are the ones that close deals in various states. Some states only use real estate attorneys, like New York and North and South Carolina. Here in

Arizona we can use title companies or attorneys, but they're a great resource for closings because they typically do not deal with the servicing side of it and will allow that to go off to a third party. So, if you use the note holder's handbook, brand it with the real estate attorney's information. Now you can offer to purchase that note shortly after closing. You can go to our website, thethrivinginvestor.com, where we have a resource guide that has all of the real estate attorneys nationwide.

The next place to look are what I call note classifieds. This is a marketplace where people sell notes. The first one would be owner will carry, that's www.ownerwillcarry.com. This is a website where people are listing a wide variety of notes for sale on a nationwide basis. Typically, they have some in every state, at all times.

Another place to look is www.fciexchange. They have both performing and nonperforming notes as well. The exchange is one that is a servicing division. They do a lot of servicing for nonperforming notes, but they also do servicing on performing notes, so they have both available at that site.

Here's one of my favorites, and if you recall, this is how I got my start in the business, 21 years ago. It is an untapped source and was very popular back then and still is today. It's placing an ad in local newspapers. 21 years ago, everything was print media. The beautiful thing today is that everything's typically online, so the classifieds are online. When people are looking through newspapers they go typically to the the digital aspect of it, but they also are printing it. When you list the ad and you put the ad together with the newspaper, you get both the print and the digital, so you've got the best of both worlds.

But you can simply put together a paying ad that would say something along these lines, "Paying top dollar for notes and mortgages, fast closings, call 555-444-3333." That's an attention getting, very cost-effective ad because it's not long, but yet it's action oriented so it gets the attention of the note seller. Keep in mind that a lot of the note sellers or the people that create notes, given that you're talking about 14 to 17% of the real estate transactions that are done with seller financing, most of them are not sophisticated in a way that know where to go sell them. So, a lot of times they are just using what I would call a common method for marketing, and this is one of those common methods. They now look through the newspaper, see your ad and ultimately give you a call. Those that do it from a digital standpoint would be seeing it in a digital form, which is still very cost effective. This works extremely well in rural areas of the country that have smaller newspapers, community newspapers and retirement community newspapers. A 30-day ad might only cost you $50.00. I only know that because living in Arizona we have a lot of retirement communities, so we reach out to them. These ads run on autopilot - you create the ad, you give them your credit card, they bill it every month or you can prepay it up front.

The next one is using free online classifieds. Go to classifiedads.com and place the same kind of ad, "Paying top dollar for notes and mortgages, fast closing, call 555-444-3333," and you can list on a nationwide digital format. I've found those to be very, very effective as well.

Another place to look are online listing sites like rentbeforeowning.com or, newrenttoownhomes.com, any of these types of sites that are offering lease purchases, land contracts, agreement for deed, contract for deed. All of those are instruments that you can purchase the same way that you would purchase a note. The only difference is on the due diligence side, and we'll get to talking about that a little bit later on in the book. This is another source for leads and an opportunity for yourself, not to mention that these sites are often evergreen, so the inventory and the opportunities are changing every day, every week, every month.

The next one is what I call bandit signs. If you're not familiar with this term, these are signs that real estate investors will place on busy corners throughout the city. They'll say, "Three bed and two bath house for sale, owner financing, call," then they give a phone number. We're looking for signs that say things like must sell fast, owner financing, phone number and then bad credit, no credit, self-employed okay.

I write down those phone numbers, I call those bandit signs and I talk to the people who have put them there and ask them what are they going to be doing with that note once they create it. Do they need help in creating something that's sellable, something that has value that they can take to the marketplace? What I'm doing is helping them to create a note that I want to purchase, but you can do the same thing. You can help them create a note that you want to purchase and that creates the type of returns that you're looking for on your investment. And by the way, these are an evergreen because they tend to be up for two or three weeks and then they disappear and here comes a new batch with a new phone number, and typically new investors to work with.

Another place to look are social sites like LinkedIn, Facebook, online real estate clubs, meet-up groups, etc. These are all key opportunities to network with people, to reach out, to let them know that you exist, that you're in the market to purchase notes. All of that is important because the bottom line is, if they don't know that you're looking to buy they don't know to offer you the opportunity. A lot of times people will take the approach, "Well, I've got a website, I've got my business card, I've got a phone number," yet people still don't know that you exist. And so the important part is letting them know that you exist and from a digital footprint, places like LinkedIn, Facebook, from online real estate clubs, it's really easy to let people know that you exist by simply writing articles that you can publish in there and putting together what we call a meme. You can put your information on that, post it in these groups, direct them back to your business site and ultimately see free traffic and inquiries and phone calls from people that are interested in selling the notes that they have.

Another place to look is through networking. You want to seek out places like realtors, title companies, attorneys, or any type of a professional networking organization or group that you attend in which they typically have meetings once a month or even once a week. Find one that has complimentary services to what you have to offer. In other words, you want to be in networking groups that have things like realtors and title companies and real estate attorneys and appraisers, developers, rehabbers, etc. Anything that has to do with real estate is going to be a good networking group for you. Then it's a matter of just attending and handing out business cards and asking if you can do a 10 or 15-minute presentation and share with them what you do and what it is that you're looking for and what kind of value you can bring to them and vice versa. We've found great success in that.

You can also offer to pay, in those networking environments, a referral fee for any business that comes your way. Referral fees can range anywhere from $100.00 to $1,000.00, all depending upon the funds in the deal and how much opportunity there is.

Next place is free print newspaper ads. This one idea was what led me to an individual that had over 700 notes for sale. As I was getting my start in the business, I didn't have a lot of money to spend on advertising. Digital media was nothing like what it is today. So, I found myself stopping at local convenience stores like Circle K and 7-Eleven and Diamond Shamrock in San Antonio, Texas. I would pick up those Thrifty Nickels and Penny Savers because they were free. I would look at the real estate section, call those people and meet with them and found out quickly that these individuals were very excited to learn how to sell their note. A lot of them were under the pretense that they were going to have to hold onto this note for 10, 20, 30 years, which was not really a part of their original plan. When I showed them that they could exit out of it, it created a tremendous amount of deal flow for our company.

The number one home run was when I contacted a gentleman from one of these ads that had 700 notes in his portfolio that he was eager to sell. I spent the next six months working with that gentleman to liquidate 38 notes that he had and I simply wholesaled them off to another institutional buyer and took a piece of the pie. Mind you, that was in the very beginning days of my career, 21 years ago.

Next, create a website for your company. Create that brand around your business, a place where people can go and find out more about you. Also, create a Facebook page and a LinkedIn profile for your company. The biggest misconception that people have in business is that because they have a phone number and a cell phone or an office address that people know who they are. The truth is, because our business is done on a nationwide basis it is virtually impossible to know everybody in the industry. So, one of the first things that we do when we get a call from somebody we are not familiar with is we will Google that person's name or that person's company and if they don't show up in LinkedIn and Facebook or they don't have a website, they tend to move down the list to the low priority.

In other words, we are really not interested in doing business with people that don't want to spend the basics on having a brand out there. LinkedIn is free, Facebook is free and a website is less than $500.00. Considering the opportunity that exists in this industry, it's easy for somebody to make seven figures a year in this industry. Spending $500.00 or $600.00 to have a website built is not that big of an expense to get into business.

The Power of Paper

This one is so simple - teach a free one-hour class to realtors. Now we are going to come back to this later on in the book, but I wanted to just kind of plant the seed here up front that if you are a realtor or if you were a realtor in the past, you know a lot about this. It is very common for them to bring in third party vendors and speakers to weekly classes that they hold at their home office. You can go in and speak in the morning, you can go in and do a lunch class, and you get an opportunity to give a 30 to 60-minute presentation. They typically will ask that you bring some kind of food. For some reason, realtors love food. So, if you bring in some boxed lunches or breakfast Danishes, the realtors will show up and actually listen to your message. They're a captive audience and when you've got the seal of approval from the broker they'll listen to your message.

You can also look at independent loan servicing companies such as Auckland. The best way is to Google loan servicing companies for a complete list of nationwide companies and then reach out and start a relationship with them. Understand, just because you called them doesn't mean that they are just going to hand you deals immediately. You need to build the relationship with them, they need to understand who you are. This is a perfect example... If you are going to be calling these people, then you're going to want a website that brands your company. You are going to want a Facebook page and a LinkedIn page because on the backside of that phone conversation, they will be googling your name and they will be googling your company information to find out who you are. If you don't show up on those search engines, they'll very quickly shoot you down and not want to do business with you because you don't have a professional online status.

Another great opportunity is to look for people with Roth IRAs. People will fill up their IRA and sometimes want to sell them off. They are looking to turn over that capital or they'll come across other investment opportunities, so they'll sell those notes off to replenish their cash in that Roth IRA. When you purchase a note from them, it will replenish their cash, parent the investment, you get the receivables on it and they get to go on to their next investment goal.

I also want to mention networking. Network with other note buyers because there are times when they need to raise capital for a lot of different reasons so therefore they'll sell off some notes. People think that we as note buyers buy and hold on to them for an indefinite period of time. Although from a principal standpoint that seems very logical, but from a reality standpoint that's not the way it happens. We buy and sell and trade on a monthly/yearly basis because we have other opportunities that require capital that we need to use, so we need to recover our capital and put it into other opportunities that are more aligned with what our goals are as a portfolio builder.

The beauty is that you've got a lot of very generous people in our industry and the majority of the industry approaches it from that perspective because it is such a huge industry dollar-wise, and the opportunities are far and above what any one person could ever acquire or manage on his or her own. So, we have a philosophy of sharing and caring about other people. We don't like to see people lose money, whether it's a competitor or a seller or anything of that nature. It's a great opportunity to sit and network and learn other strategies, ideas, game plans, overcoming hurdles, how to partner, etc.

Last but not least is mortgage companies. Every mortgage company has loans that they can't sell to Wall Street because they don't meet compliance rules and guidelines. They are also known in the industry as what we call scratch and dent loans. It's not that the loans are non-enforceable, it's just that because of the banking institutions and Wall Street and the various rules and regulations that they have to comply with, they ultimately end up overlooking very minor details in a loan that have massive impact on whether or not they can sell it. Such as they didn't get one of the borrowers to sign the last page of the credit application or the 1003, they didn't do a desk review on the appraisal, the credit was pulled outside of the time that was allotted, the Truth in Lending has the wrong date on it, it's three days older than it should be, and so forth.

These types of things are very specific details that the financial institutional world looks at and turns their nose up and walks away from a deal of that nature because when they're purchasing loans and they're pooling them together they want to get an "X" level. They want to get a certain level of credit rating on that portfolio or that mortgage backed security, which is what they're really attempting to do. If they have flaws in a loan, then that lowers their credit rating or their grade, so they won't take that on because it could be the difference of tens of thousands of dollars, or even millions of dollars in a multi-billion-dollar transaction.

The beautiful thing for you and me as street level investors is that we can buy those loans at nice discounts and they are full package loans, they are institutional quality and ultimately, they will sell them off to you or me at a discount. And the reason they sell them off is because every mortgage company has what they call a warehouse line. The warehouse line is designed to hold loans for a 90-day period of time. Any time a loan goes past that 90-day period it changes the cost of the capital on that warehouse line, so they don't want to run that risk.

If somebody or something falls behind, now they need to figure out a different strategy for that borrower or that particular loan because they ultimately made an error on that loan, so now they are willing to discount it to get it off their line of credit. These are called 'scratch and dents.' We see them on a regular basis throughout our industry, through our office, and they're full dock loans, institutional quality that we can buy at discount.

The reason I've shared the number of different ideas here is that they all work very well. However, I also understand that the readership of this book comes from a lot of different experiences, from a lot of different industries, from a lot of different opportunities. If you were once a mortgage broker, it might be a great thing to reach out to those coworkers that you previously worked with because you will have a quicker inroad to reaching out to other mortgage companies about this one particular idea.

Chapter 3

Due Diligence

When we first see a note, there's some basic information that we want to gather in the beginning. One of the things is the terms of the deal. In other words, the sales price, down payment, note amount, first payment due date and interest rate, (whether it's a principal interest payment or it's an interest only payment, whether it's 10, 20, 30 years, if it has a balloon or not, etc.) We also want to find out whether or not it's owner occupied, or non-owner occupied, and I'm speaking to the residential side of the business. These are some basic things that we want to gather right out of the gate.

There are some sellers who are knowledgeable and understand they're going to be selling the note at a discount. You've got some people that have kind of a gray idea about whether or not they can sell it at a discount, but they just don't know what that discount is. In other words, a lot of times they think it's a huge discount which is the opposite end of the note buying spectrum. And then you've got sellers that want par, meaning they want the full-face amount of the note.

There's challenges with each one of those sellers. The person that wants par or the full-face amount of the note are often basing their idea on a particular rate of return or the interest rate of the note, meaning if the note has an 8% interest rate they oftentimes try and compare it to a CD or a money market account and even the stock market as a way of "establishing that this has more value than those other methods." The fundamental challenge is those notes, when sold based on that premise, lack stability. Meaning they lack stability in the borrower and that's true for all three of those groups.

You always have to keep in mind that when we are buying the note or investing in the note, that these people were not institutional quality people for one reason or another. I'm not saying that means that they are bad people. It just means that the banks and institutions didn't want to lend them money for some reason. In the world of investing, the number one thing you want to do is preserve capital. You don't want to just be investing for the sake of investing because the moment the note stops paying, whatever your yield is, it goes to zero. Now all of a sudden, you've got a cost of capital that far exceeds your rate of return.

That being said, oftentimes those people that are selling at par pricing or full-face value are unaware of the challenges that lay on the backside of the note. They think because you're getting 8% that that is a great idea. It works well for them. It doesn't work well for an investor in the event that the note goes into default, which is a possibility. Keep in mind, for one reason or another, most seller finance notes start to default around 36 months, for one reason or another and so you have to keep that in mind. So that's Category One, meaning they want par.

Category 2, the other side of the spectrum, is where sellers think that all they are going to get is 10 or 20 cents on the dollar, which is not always accurate. Those types of sellers are often fearful that they are going to get involved in a transaction and ultimately somewhere down the road, somebody's going to change the price on the deal and they're not going to get anywhere close to what was promised in the beginning. Although we have never seen that happen around our office, I have heard of it happening in the industry.

Those people are looking at stability when they sell the note and they are looking at something more reasonable, but they've got this idea in their mind that it should be something or all anybody's going to offer them is 10 cents, 20 cents, 30 cents on the dollar. The truth is when we purchase a note, what we are really looking for is stability in the borrower, a fair rate of return on our money, and longevity as far as a passive income on our investment.

Category 3 is when you get sellers that are very reasonable in their pricing model and they understand it. They have done it maybe a time or two and what they are really looking to do is to become more proficient at it so that they can do more notes in their business and use it as a financing division inside of their fix and flip or fix and rehab or rehab and sell business model that they are currently involved in.

We actually enjoy working with all three groups, but the last group is one that ultimately brings us a substantial amount of business because if we can help them grow their business by creating better quality notes, then that creates more business for us. It creates a better business for them and it helps out more homeowners going forward.

We like to look at notes prior to the note being signed or any kind of legal binding contract being signed where we can go in and do a pre-due diligence, or what we call pre-underwriting, for the note seller and let him or her know that what they are creating or the direction they're going in is going to help them accomplish their goal, or if we need to modify the terms of the note so that they can ultimately accomplish their goal.

We are able to see what kind of borrower we are working with, what kind of down payment we're working with, what type of property we are working with. Is it fully rehabbed? Is it more of a cosmetic rehab? We get to see the terms of the deal upfront so if we need to tweak the terms a little bit, we can. Maybe instead of doing a 5% rate we do a 7% rate, something that will ultimately balance out the loan so that it's a very reasonable, fair and affordable loan for the homeowner. We also want to help the note seller accomplish his or her financial goal, as well as create a higher quality product for us to purchase in the end.

We have been doing that and offering that as a service to clients for close to 15 years now and we still offer that today. The great part about that is we can also tell a note seller, "Hey, don't sell this house to this person because of a, b, c, or d." It might be poor credit, no money down the fact that they don't have a job, they can't afford it, things of that nature. It helps them avoid a pitfall and it helps them to avoid getting into any kind of a legal binding contract that ultimately causes them financial harm down the road.

So, for some people in the business and some people who buy homes, sometimes their desire to want to buy a home is not necessarily the best thing for them to be doing. Maybe they need to save a little more for their down payment. Maybe they need to work on cleaning up their credit. Maybe they haven't been on their job long enough. Maybe they need to find a job or a better paying job so that they have the finances to be able to afford the property so that when they do enter into the agreement, all parties are participating to the highest level possible.

Although I believe everybody should have an opportunity to purchase a home, I don't believe that everybody has the right to purchase a home. Not every opportunity that comes across their desk is the right timing for them to purchase a home either. The thing that note or property sellers have to keep in mind is that when they are entering into these contracts, into these agreements, just because there's a dollar amount on the note, it doesn't necessarily mean that that note is worth that, primarily because of what it is backed by. It's backed by two key elements. One is the homeowner's ability to repay, as well as the quality of the homeowner based on their credit. Number two, the property itself based on loan to value.

So, as a note investor, these are the types of things that we look at when we are working with a note seller. We are not a yield driven buyer, meaning I would buy a note at an 8% yield over a note with a 12% yield just because the borrower is a higher quality borrower or they put more money down or the quality of the property is there. What we don't want to do is buy properties or notes on properties where the borrower doesn't have any money down or they have less than 10% down. These are key elements to keep in mind as well. When you're working with a buyer, a simple rule of thumb to follow is 10% down, 10, 20, 30-year terms, a credit score of 575 or better and an interest rate somewhere between 6 to 9% with no prepayment penalty. Now that's what I call the center lane of the highway. That is the part of the freeway where you can play safe, majority of deals can fit within that parameter and you can crank those deals out and you can duplicate that model over and over and over again.

Credit

Credit plays a big role when it comes to notes. You still have to have good credit, and we look at this in length. What's driving this person's credit down? Is it the fact they went through a tough season and they haven't taken time to re-establish credit? Are the issues on their credit old issues? Are they recent issues? Are they medical issues? Are they credit card issues? Are they child support issues? What's actually doing the damage that is bringing the credit score down? Is it something that they can easily rectify? If they had an extra $1,500, could they pay off these three or four accounts which would in turn raise their credit score? The point being is that most of these things are very solvable challenges with a home buyer.

The question then becomes if they are willing to do the deal. Is the note seller willing to help them or are we just buying it as is? Because ultimately notes are sold as is. There are no reps, there are no warrants. When we purchase it, we purchase it in its entirety. We can do partials, but even partials are purchased in their entirety. With that being said, now we've got full responsibility over that particular investment and with that we now have to understand we are actually investing in, meaning that homeowner, that particular property, and his or her ability to repay us in a timely fashion.

It has never been our goal in business to take somebody's property. That is not a model to us at any level. That is a costly, expensive, time consuming legal hassle that is part of the industry, but it shouldn't be the main part of the industry. That is always something that we strive to address in the early stages of reviewing a note deal. Now no matter which category of a seller we are working with, whether it's somebody that wants par or somebody who thinks they'll only get 20 cents on the dollar, or somebody that's very reasonable and has done a couple of deals, one of the things we always want to see on the front side is the borrower's credit.

The easiest indicator to determining the value of the note is a borrower's credit, not to mention you can get a copy of their credit relatively easy and relatively inexpensive. That is a key element just like everything else that we deal with as consumers. One of the first things any creditor wants to know about you and me or anybody else is what our credit is so that they know if or how to work with us within our request, whether that's buying a cellphone, getting health insurance, buying a house, a car, etc.

So, when we are first talking with a seller, we want to get the basic numbers of the deal. We want to get a copy of the borrower's credit and then we have a little in-house mortgage worksheet that we use, and we fill it out or the seller can fill it out. We actually prefer that the seller fills it out, so it is more accurate and we don't overlook something and make an honest mistake. But with that, we can in turn determine whether or not this is a deal that we can work with and help that seller accomplish that goal.

The Power of Paper

Now why do we do it that way? Well, it's simple. We do it that way because we want to put the best pricing possible and the most honest and accurate pricing possible upfront and on the table. What happens a lot of times is people will overprice the deal only to find out two weeks later that the borrower's credit is not a 640, it's a 550. Now they have to change the offer and ultimately that doesn't sit well with sellers. It doesn't sit well with anybody involved in the deal and I see most of the time those deals fall apart and they never get done because now the trust between the parties has been breached and broken and now nobody wants to work with each other. Or if they do work with each other, they work with each other to get the deal done and then they never do business again.

Now, there's a lot of flaws in that. I'm not saying one party is better than the other when you're dealing with a buyer and seller doing it that way. I have just learned after 21 years that if you can get some really high-quality information upfront, more accurate information, that ultimately, you're going to have a more accurate quote and have a much smoother deal from beginning to end.

The other side of that equation is we want to make sure, especially on newly created deals, that the home buyer has the ability to repay. We want to look at their debt to income ratio. We want to make sure that they are not making $3,000 a month and their mortgage payment is $1,500 a month. That's not a debt ratio that we can live with. What we're typically looking to do, and although we can actually go above this, we like to keep the debt to income ratio right around 36 to 38%. We have found that that's a very comfortable ratio for the homeowner. It's also a very comfortable ratio for us and it helps us to avoid any future defects in the note and any future foreclosure possibilities associated with that note.

Now, once the deal is done, meaning that it is a seasoned deal, say one or two payments, we can't change the terms of the deal but we can still look at their debt to income ratio on the deal to determine whether or not that's a deal that we would want to purchase. We usually do that through looking at a 1003. We encourage all sellers to get a 1003, fill it out and then have that on file internally and use it for their own debt to income ratio as well.

A 1003 is a standard industry credit application. Most people have seen them if they have gone and applied for a mortgage loan at a bank or a mortgage broker and you can easily get one by going online. In that 1003, you will see everything from the address of the property, the type of property, the borrower's information, the co-borrower's information meaning name, address, social security number, job information. It also gets into their liabilities, into their assets, what their current rent or mortgage is, what their proposed mortgage is going to be. It gets into several questions about foreclosures and bankruptcies. So, it's an all-inclusive credit application that once the note holder has that, they have very extensive information on that borrower which helps them to put together a higher quality file.

One of the most important parts of creating a high-quality note has everything to do with the information that the note holder gathers on the borrower. Meaning that when you're creating a mortgage or a note or carrying back a note or mortgage on a property, you want to make sure that you have a 1003 on that borrower or borrowers, if there is more than one. You want to make sure you have scored credit reports from all three bureaus for every person that is listed on the loan. You want to make sure that their debt to income ratio is in line. We also want to make sure that you have a lender's title policy. Pay the extra hundred dollars and give them an owner's title policy. Make sure that the loan is closed through a title company or a law firm, whichever applies to where the property is located.

The Power of Paper

You want to make sure that you have an appraisal, either a drive by or a full appraisal. Now, people often balk at that idea, but here's why. If you just base the sales price of a property off of a BPO, or some constant you got from a friend of a friend who's a realtor friend type thing, that doesn't really give the true accurate value of that property. Paying an appraiser anywhere from $250 to a drive by to $450 for a full appraisal will increase the value of that property anywhere from 2 to 10%. That 2 to 10% increase in value can also apply to an increase in sales price on that property.

I coach and encourage people to do that prior to putting the house on the market. Now why do I say that? Well one, if you're going to do a full appraisal, which I highly recommend, you can get the appraiser on the property based on your timeline and their timeline and you're not at the mercy of a homeowner. The appraiser can go in there and take all the photographs they need. They can do all the measurements they need so they have tremendous accuracy. Especially if you're remodeling a house and you have added square footage, you absolutely want to do that.

That only benefits you as a seller and it only benefits them as a borrower because you can get the appraisal in a PDF and give them a copy of it at the closing table, which also helps to solidify and substantiate your sales price because when you're selling via owner financing you don't want to extend a discount on the value of your property. In other words, if somebody comes up to you and wants you to do sell financing and you are selling your house for $150,000 but now they only want to pay $140,000 and it's worth $150,000 because you have an appraisal, sell it for $150,000. Don't sell it for $1400,000. Create a note and take a discount on the note as well. That means you have taken a double discount on it. It also doesn't help them as a home buyer. If they want the $140,000 sales price, encourage them to go get institutional financing and pay you the $140,000. Most people would be more than happy to take $140,000 cash on a $150,000 home.

I want to mention here, too, that a lot of time sellers will be able to sell the house for more than market value because they are offering a desperate buyer owner financing and the note holders got to protect himself from that. We have seen that happen on many occasions where the opposite happens. We get note sellers, note holders, who sell the property for less than it's really worth and we like those deals. We get note holders that sell the property for exactly what it's worth with an appraisal and then we get note holders that sell it for more than it's worth. What I tell those people that do it for more than it's worth is that when they do that, we're going to base our value off of the lower of the two.

In other words, if they've sold a $150,000 house for $160,000, that house is only worth $150,000 with that homeowner putting down $15,000 cash. That ultimately means they are at about a 95% loan to value, which will impact our pricing to the note holder. In other words, our pricing just gets lower. So even though they sold it for more doesn't mean that they are going to get more. It means that we back off our pricing because the risk factor increases there.

How does it increase? Well very simple. If you sell somebody something for more than it's worth, and in real estate it happens quite a bit, then that homeowner or that property owner will eventually figure that out. Whether that's talking to a real estate friend, have it appraised or talking to a neighbor, the minute they figure out that they overpaid for a property and that they were cheated out of their money, they will start creating problems because they were taken advantage of. We know that because we have seen it happen time and time again with those types of deals.

Ultimately, what we find ourselves doing when we buy those types of deals is going in there and modifying the loan early on so that in fact that doesn't happen. Because once again, we are looking at just the cash flow aspect of it. We don't want to deal with legal issues. We don't want to be going to court and fighting over the 'he said, she said' aspects of the business. I encourage people to not oversell their property. I encourage them to sell it for what its true market value is and not a penny less, but not a penny more. Whatever it is, it is. That way they trade a very clean deal that all of their numbers speak to and cater to.

Home Inspections

We talked about the credit. We talked about the debt to income. We talked about the value. Another important part to do, especially with property owners and the amount of rehabbing and the amount of fix and flip companies out there that are doing amazing work and really revitalizing neighborhoods, is to go in and do an inspection on the property.

Now, the primary reason for that is one, it makes sure that everything that they have done to that property is up to code, so it covers themselves as well as the homeowner. Paying that minimal amount of money is a lot cheaper than dealing with issues 30, 60 or 90 days after you close on the property and then you find electrical issues or plumbing issues or roofing issues because things got overlooked or they weren't up to code.

Now, I know that some people out there completely disagree with me on this point but I've seen those types of issues get ignored. If people ignore those issues, what happens is even if they sell the note, whoever buys that note will not want to do business with that note seller ever again because they inherited a problem. They invested for long-term residual value, but they inherited a huge problem and they paid a premium to inherit that problem. That's just not the model that we are looking for. That's not the type of business that we do.

With that, if you do the inspection, not only does it protect the property seller and note holder, but it also protects the property buyer. You can deal with and address any issues that may come up in an inspection report and make sure that it's all signed off and cleaned up and cleared up. Most note sellers think that the cost factor for these repairs has to come out of their pocket, but it doesn't have to. These things can be paid for by the home buyer and under any normal circumstances would be paid for by the home buyer.

We just recently sold a home and the buyer paid for their own inspection. They paid for their own appraisal. They had the mortgage company and people doing those things for them. You can assist your buyer in doing the same thing which clears and cleans up any kind of questions or issues that may not have been immediately present. It also creates a much cleaner deal and it creates a higher quality deal for a note buyer.

Keep in mind that no matter what yield a note buyer buys at, whether it is 5%, 6%, 15%, 20%, it doesn't matter. The minute that borrower stops paying, that yield goes to zero. That is in fact what they are looking to avoid. They don't want it to go to zero. They want it to be whatever level the parties have agreed to and they want it to be a hands-off, turn-key residual income model. That's how they view it. And the closer that you can create that model for a note investor, the cleaner your deals are, the faster they will get closed, the more money you are going to get for them. That means you will be able to turn that money more times in a calendar year and use it on other projects and properties which means that you or a note holder will absolutely make more money every year.

Avoiding those little, tiny things create more problems than they solve.

This is a sermon that I have been preaching for years. It's much like those that rehab homes; the challenge there is that for years they just used to do laminate and other low-cost items. Then people started putting in tile and getting more money for their houses and putting in a better carpet and getting more money for their houses. Then they figured out, "I've got to do that because my competition's doing that." Then they started putting in granite countertops and other high-end items. The industry changed over the years, so they needed to change.

Well, the same thing happened with the note industry. It's changed. It's matured. It's gotten better over time and note sellers have to keep their finger on the pulse to know what's important to have when they are creating these notes. Otherwise, they are just flying by the seat of their pants, spending a lot of extra time trying to find the right buyer. They are going to spend a lot of extra time in due diligence. They are going to spend a lot of extra time gathering things that they forgot. They are going to spend a lot of extra time building and putting together the file that they didn't know they needed to put together. They are going to spend a lot of extra time and money getting things like title work and legal docs and things of that nature put together as well because these are things they just didn't know about. They just didn't know what they didn't know. Not that there's any ethical issues here. It's just that they just didn't know.

Location

One of the things that's important to understand is that we see a lot of different neighborhoods. Some are more desirable than others. There's great opportunity for investors, as well as note investors in those neighborhoods. The thing that we're looking is the overall quality of the neighborhood. Is it seeing an increase in value? Is it seeing a decrease in value?

We are also looking at the overall quality of the house, as well as its neighbors. If it is a stand-alone house on a street full of empty lots and there are cars on blocks in the street, then it is probably not going to be a deal that we are interested in. But if it's a house that's on a street of houses and are in various levels of condition and people are living in these houses then that's not going to scare us away.

We have seen on several occasions where people will go out and take pictures, what we call "street scenes" and catch issues in the photographs, like people doing drug deals in the middle of the street or cars casing the area. These are not the type of neighborhoods we really want to be in. But when it's just blatant and in our face, that is not something we are really interested in.

We look at the surrounding area of the neighborhood. What's the grading on the school district? Are there churches? Are there shopping centers? Are there grocery stores? Are there convenience stores? Are there freeways close by? What's the zip code value, meaning the overall average value? What's the overall average income in the neighborhood? These are all key factors of the due diligence that we do on the backside of the note to make sure that we're buying something that is ultimately going to be repaid.

We don't shy away from houses in these types of areas. What we do is we want to make sure that that borrower, once again going back to their employment, their 1003, their credit and things of that nature, that that borrower has been set up for success. Success not only in their personal life but also success in the fact that they are going to be able to repay us in a timely fashion or in a fashion that we agree to or that is consistent to the loan documents.

What we have seen as a trend in our industry over the last 12 months is that home values and home prices keep going up. I'm not saying that we're back to pre-2007 prices, but what we are seeing is a general trend, which is a positive thing because it is an indicator that neighborhoods are getting back on their feet. That is an indicator that all of these investors that have been remodeling homes nationwide are having a major impact in a very positive way of cleaning up and revitalizing neighborhoods. That is a great thing. Those things are key to not only creating higher quality product, but also better neighborhoods, better housing, better communities for everybody, no matter what income level they operate at or live at.

We have seen that the average unpaid principal balance of our portfolio has now creeped up into the 170 range, whereas before it was around the 120 range, which is another positive thing. We have found that as home values go up, people who cannot get the higher priced homes are just staying with being in the rental market. Another key element that we look at when we buy notes is how many homes are rental homes in the area. If it's over 43% we tend to shy away from those types of seller financed deals. We also don't like what we call concentrated areas, meaning if there is a note on a condo or a townhouse and more than 40% of that community is rental properties, we are not interested in that note either because ultimately that property could be a rental property. Not to mention that rental properties tend to be less taken care of, as opposed to a property that is personally owned.

So those are some key elements that we look at when we are looking at notes to purchase as we look at the neighborhood: we look at the zip code, we look at the school district, we look at the income, we look at the demographics, we look at the location and its proximity to freeways. We look at the rental properties in the neighborhood. All of those things are imperative to making sure that we are buying something that is in a high-quality area.

The whole reason for doing due diligence goes back to the fact that we are lifestyle investors here at Pinnacle Investments. We buy things that create residual income. We buy things that put our money to work for us so that it spins off a return that minimizes our risk and minimizes our efforts in that particular investment. It also minimizes our cost overall.

If you end up as an investor and buy notes in rougher areas, as we do, chances are they will default, which will have a negative impact on your portfolio, driving down the overall quality of the investments. This means that you start incurring all kinds of additional costs that are over and above what you want to be dealing with as a passive investor.

Chapter 4

Servicing and Creating a Better Product

Back in the old days, some 21 years ago, servicing certainly wasn't what it is today, in regard to the rules and regulations. There was a lot more freedom for people to basically manage their own portfolio, manage their own investments and to control them. There were a lot of positives in that and one of them being it was much more personal, meaning that when you invested in the note, you typically got to know the homeowner. The homeowner would call you up on a good old fashioned 1-800 number and talk to you if there were any issues or challenges, like making their payment. But a lot of times, especially if you were in the local area, you would often have someone stop by your office and pay you in cash, and the cash often ended up in the pockets of the investor or a family safe or even a desk drawer, for that matter. It wasn't really accounted for.

There really wasn't an accounting method that they followed, outside of maybe a simple amortization schedule that they would print off. And then, they would just check off the payment. They wouldn't issue the old 1098 year-end interest payment statements, or anything of that nature to the homeowner either, which is a very important part of the business.

Oftentimes, when you would buy notes and you would request a payment history, you would get copies of $100 bills, or $50 bills, or $20, or a variety of these bills, and that would be considered payment, and that investor, that seller, would ultimately pull that money of out of their pocket, put it on a table, take a photocopy of it and send it, and that constituted a payment. So, I would say there was a lot of gray areas in the business 21 years ago.

We also relied heavily on things like Gestapo letters. This is where we would send a letter out to the homeowner, verifying their current balance on the loan, and if they didn't respond within 10 days it was considered valid and accurate. And we still use that technique in today's marketplace. One of the other things that we dealt with in the servicing industry was things like down payments; either people not having down payment money, or they would give the down payment to the investor and the investor wouldn't give it to the title company, resulting in the title company not putting it on the closing statement.

There were all these gray areas even as far as the notes were written. I have seen many deals where the note was handwritten on a napkin. I saw several on yellow notebook paper and that constituted a legal binding contract in the space, so there's a lot of freedom. There was a lot of wiggle room, a lot of gentleman's agreements, a lot of trust, and a lot of opportunity to not necessarily be so accurate with numbers and things of that nature.

The bad side of that was that people took advantage of those things. Oftentimes, we ran into issues where the homeowner would get a refund on their tax return and would apply that towards their principal balance, or we find out that the homeowner was making double payments and not getting full credit. Lower income people is where we saw a lot of that abuse. These people were hard working, and they were doing the right thing for them, and that was paying off their mortgage and aggressively getting after it, and then, not getting full credit for it. They oftentimes payed in cash, which unfortunately wasn't traceable.

Investing in notes was either something done by the elite, or what I would call a professional investor. And now, it's become more mainstream in the marketplace, where you've got people that are looking to invest in notes as a form of residual income, and they've got their money spread out in a multitude of investments: gold, silver, stock, bonds, etc. The industry, unfortunately, has cleaned itself up. We had some major players come into the marketplace, as well as some big money. Major players like the Associates Financial Services (they were backed by Ford Motor Corporation), MetLife, CBass, and Note One. All of these people came into the marketplace and some of them are still very much a part of it, and they demanded that the industry clean itself up.

But, they unfortunately changed up their underwriting guidelines, which forced people to comply. Complying means that if you are selling a house and you receive money as a down payment, you need to make sure that the down payment not only gets written into the paperwork, but that a receipt is given to them from the title company so that they get full credit for that deposit.

In the past, an investor would take the money, put it in their pocket, and forget to give the home buyer that deposit. Mind you, these were typically on deals that were less than $50,000, which was a big part of the marketplace 21 years ago. Now, the market place has elevated itself and is now dealing with six figure homes, so the culture and the clientele is a lot different. Point being, the note sellers wanted more money for the notes, which is reasonable and understandable, the buyer said, "Okay, if you want more money, then we want a better product. We want a higher quality product. We want a product that we can board into our portfolio, which will enhance our portfolio. So, this is what we need you guys to do: quit putting the down payment in your pocket and quit accepting cash from these buyers. Even if they're in your local area and they're coming in to your office to make the payment, have them give you a check, money order or a cashier's check which can be photocopied. This will track the buyer's payment history and give them proper credit for principal and interest payments according to the note, and according to how they pay. This will connect the dots digitally for you."

If the homeowner pays extra, maybe they make two payments, maybe they do a principal reduction payment, or something along those lines, make sure that is allocated for and that it is also in their pay history.

At the end of the year, as an investor, you're collecting interest, and that interest is considered income on that investment, so you have to issue a 1098. It's required by IRS law, and the buyers were saying, "You need to issue these year-end statements because of two things: One, you're receiving interest income and number two, it is the single largest tax deduction for the majority of US homeowners in the country." No matter what your income level is, that tends to be one of the largest single item tax deductions that they have, and that could be the difference between the borrower getting a refund or paying taxes. Not to mention, it's required by IRS law to have that happen as well.

So, the beauty behind this is the industry started out more of a hobby/good old boy type of business back in the '60s, '70s, and '80s and it allowed the average investor to start developing long term individual wealth without all the heavy lifting that goes with rental income. But because there were no real guidelines, and there was no real manual or book, people kind of made up their own rules as they went along. I would say that the majority of the rules they made up were really good, but there were some that had a tendency to operate more in the gray, and some were just blatantly fraud.

It was just a big mess. They were buying stuff and having to clean it up, fill in the gaps, bring in additional documentation, and reinvent or rebuild the loan with the homeowner in place. They were having to do all this extra work, when at the same time, the investors were saying, "Give me more money." In any economic model, if somebody wants more money for something, then they have to produce a better product in order to achieve that, no matter what the model is. So, the industry came back and said, "Okay, Mr. Note Sellers, we need you guys to produce a better product, and if you produce a better product, then we'll give you more money for it."

So, the industry started self-managing and self-guiding and cleaning itself up by closing at title companies, getting title policies, getting full appraisals versus just drive-by appraisals, having insurance on the properties and making sure taxes were paid up on the properties. The paperwork was produced by either legal counsel or by an account or someone who had the professional skill to do so. It was much more inclusive. There were more disclosures added to the file, which is good for both the homeowner and the investor. Then, the people even went as far as to start hiring professional servicing companies to collect the payments for them. Ultimately, people started realizing that if they wanted to make more money, they had to produce a better product.

People started developing other sub-culture businesses, or sub-businesses, like servicing companies and servicing entities. Some of them had been around forever, but they weren't really marketing, so they got into the marketing craze and started letting people know, "hey, here we are. We can help you." One of those places would be Note Servicing Center, which has been around for 30 years. They work with a lot of investors on performing notes, and they do an amazing job of it. The great thing about having a third-party company service a person's notes, or service the investment, is that they handle over 90% of it.

The beauty of that is they are collecting the payments, they are making sure that the payments are being applied properly. They are making sure that if the borrower makes an extra payment that it gets applied properly. They are making sure that the taxes are paid on the property, that the insurance is in place, that the year-end interest statements are issued and sent out to all of the homeowners so that they get proper credit. They are staying in compliance with IRS law as well as other state and federal laws around the country.

The truth about today's noted investors is that they need and must use a servicing company to service their notes.

Now, for those of you out there reading this book right now, you are probably wondering why that is. The truth is that the federal government realized that because there were some gray areas in our industry, they needed to come in and set up rules. Those rules and laws demand that we, as investors, use servicing companies that are licensed in the state the property resides in, not the state we do business in. To service our loans, we have a third-party individual that basically manages the relationship for both sides, the investor and the homeowner.

The great part about that is that the service isn't overly expensive, around $15 a month per loan. It's a very small price to pay to remain in compliance and it's a very small price to pay to make sure that your accounting records are in line with both state and federal guidelines.

So, today, as an investor, when I buy a note from an individual, not only am I going through and doing my normal due diligence, but one of the parts of that due diligence is making sure that the homeowner has gotten proper credit for the payments that they have made throughout the life of the loan, and we do that by one, running a fresh amortization schedule, based on the terms of the note, and then, matching that up with the payments that have been made, and the copies of the payments that have been provided.

Then, we will even send out a letter to the homeowner letting him know this is what we calculated, this is how many payments we show that you have made, this is when we started, this is what's due next, are you in agreement? Very seldom do we have any pushback on it.

Technology has helped the industry grow. It has given investors more tools and resources to streamline the business. The advancement on technology, the demand in the marketplace for a better product, the demand in the marketplace for higher pricing, all this inevitably forced the buyers and the sellers to create a better product.

The Power of Paper

Chapter 5

Servicing in Today's Era

Let's fast forwarded to 2017. We now have reforms in place like Dodd-Frank that have come along and added additional regulations to the marketplace, including forcing us to use servicing companies. Now, some people have a lot of pushback on that. I, personally, think it's phenomenal. One, it keeps everybody out of trouble. Two, it protects the borrower. Three, it protects the investor, so it's a win-win-win. It's a very, very small cost to maintain that level, or that peace of mind with every investment that you make, so in boarding a loan with a servicer or servicing company like Note Servicing Center, it's really a very easy process.

Number one, they charge a small boarding fee. Typically, it's around $25 per loan for you to board it. Number two, they ask for an information sheet on that particular borrower. Number three, they want particular pieces of documentation like a copy of the note, amortization schedules, pay history, things of that nature. They put a fresh set of eyes on it to make sure that everything lines up.

Now, 97% of the time, everything is status quo. You do get that 3% where somebody makes advanced payments, falls behind, accrues some late fees, or even has bounced check fees. You can forgive that as an investor and reset the loan, based on just the UPB, and forgive those things that may have been lingering out there and technically are owed. Usually you find doing that is really a blessing and gets the relationship between you and the homeowner off on the right foot, because you can put it in the form of a letter to them, and that comes out of the audit that is done on the file when you board it in with somebody like Note Servicing Center.

So, they will go in and do a light audit of the file, and with that, they make sure their numbers match up with our numbers and the seller's numbers, and if there's a discrepancy, then we'll cross that bridge when we get there. Discrepancies are typically late fees, additional interest, bounced check charges. But you have the ability to just forgive those things as a note investor, and put that in the form of a letter to the home owner, and you find that they're very gracious, which gets the relationship off on the right foot.

Once you fill out their intake form, the loan is boarded with a particular servicing company. What I like about Note Center is you can track your loans through a portal, so you have the ability to track online for payments, etc., so you know who's paying and who's not paying, and who might need an extra call or push. Once that loan is boarded and it is up and running, a "hi, bye" letter is sent out to the homeowner, letting him or her know they have 15 days to respond. However, you are also letting him know that as of a future date, that that homeowner will be sending their payments to a new collection center, or what we call a "drop box" in the industry.

So, let's say I was to buy, as an investor, a note on October 1st, and we closed the deal on October 1st. Now, I may have been doing due diligence on that note since July or August, or I may have just been doing it for two weeks. Point being, the closing date of the loan is what matters; for this example, the closing date being October 1st. Well, there'd be a goodbye letter that's also dated for October 1st, which is then mailed out to that homeowner, letting them know that their November payment is going to be mailed to a new mailing address. It also reassures them that there are no changes to their loan, with the exception of the mailing address.

The dollar amount doesn't change, but the mailing address and who they make the check out to do change. They make the check out to a new company, which in this case would be Pinnacle Investments, or Note Servicing Center on behalf of Pinnacle Investments, and then they mail it to a new address, or a new drop box. The terms, the conditions, the unpaid principal balance remain the same. Whatever it was, it was. The October 1st payment would still be owed that to the original note holder.

Federal law requires a 15-day notice. If you date the letter October 1st, 15 days which would technically be October 16th, but their next payment's not due until November 1st, so you've given them plenty of notice where to send their November payment. Now, that's a requirement by federal law to be mailed out to each and every note or payer on a note, and not only is it a requirement, but it's also just a good habit.

We were doing it voluntarily for 21 years, and all of a sudden, it just became a law. Once it became a law, it just became a little more rigid with the 15-day notice. Outside of that, nothing changes for the homeowner. They get full credit. All the payments that were collected from January to October 1st, the responsibility of issuing that year-end tax statement or 1098 is the responsibility of the previous owner.

Being an owner, I will issue one for November and December of that year, and then, will continue on the following year, as long as I own it. Here's the beauty of that. A servicing company will do all of those things. They can even mail out the goodbye letter, but I usually have it as part of my closing package because it's faster and easier. I want to make sure that we're as efficient as humanly possible and making sure that we're getting things out to people as quickly as possible. That way they have enough notice. If they have any questions they can reach out to us on our 1-800 number, where we can introduce ourselves.

We typically will follow up with an introduction call to that homeowner and let them know who we are, what our plans are and what our intentions are. We will also do a payer interview with that homeowner to go over things that they love about the house, things that they've done to the house, and things that they would like to change about the house. What do they love about the neighborhood? Is everybody still working? Has everybody been on their jobs for X amount of time? In other words, we want to get to know the payer. We also want them to have a comfort level with us as well, so we provide them with our 1-800 number. Now, why do we do this?

It's very important so they know who we are, and we know who they are, but it's even more important that to give them permission to call us in the event that something is delayed on their payment is establishing a baseline for communication between our firm and the homeowner. That way, the homeowner knows that we're here to help them, we're here to support them, but we also have a legal binding agreement that needs to be managed and complied throughout the remaining portion of the relationship.

Now, this goes into another part of the business.

The biggest thing to remember when you buy a note is you are the new owner of it, you are typically buying a note that's outside of your state or your home town. It's very common for us to buy notes all over the country. We buy some in Phoenix, but we don't just focus in Phoenix. because we are looking for deals that make financial sense. And not every deal in Phoenix makes financial sense any more than any deal in Dallas, Texas, or Miami, Florida, for that matter. One of the most important things that you can do when you buy a new loan, and you've introduced yourself to the homeowner and you have done the payer interview, and you have done all of the things that you wanted to do in regard to educating them on who you are and what you're about, is you want to make sure that you establish boundaries.

The Power of Paper

If the payment of the note is due the first of the month, and you don't have that payment in your drop box or in your account or in your office because they accidentally sent it to our office versus to the servicing company, we just simply forward it on to the servicing company. We don't put it in our bank account. We forward it on so that it has proper credit, and then, they'll forward the money back to us.

The reason we do that when those things happen is we want to make sure that we are adding value to that file. One of the biggest things that adds value to a note, especially a seasoned note, is quality seasoning, meaning that if I want to sell that loan, a year, two years, three years from now, I want to make sure that there's an accurate accounting of every single payment that was made, and that there's no gaps or questions in the accounting ledger sheet. So if I keep that payment, now there's a gap. Then, I have to explain why I kept the payment, rather than just sending it on to the servicing company, waiving the late fee on it, because I can do that, and having them apply it, because we did receive it. We just received it at the wrong address.

Because we are both on the same team, we will allow those things. We will give grace on those types of things. The point being is that two years from now, 18 months from now, whenever it might be, when I go to sell that loan, I can easily go to the account and print off the pay history and add that to the file and whoever the new buyer is, they can look at it, and say, "This is a stellar pay history. This homeowner is on track." They see that, and they believe that because it's done by third party. You've got a third-party servicing agency that's handling it, so it's really, really hard to commit fraud or to cook the books. When that happens, and it will, you want to make sure that you forward it on.

Now, the other side of that coin, let's say it's November 5th, and you still haven't received your payment. You need to pick up the phone. You need to send out a late letter on the 2nd, because technically speaking, all of us are in default on our loan if the payment is not there on the 1st. This is written on every mortgage out there, whether it's institutional or seller financed.

I know some of you out there are saying, "But wait a minute. I have a 10-day grace period. I have a five-day grace period. I have a 15-day grace period." You're right. You do. So do I. But, legally, you're in default when you miss the payment date. Now, they give a grace period for things like pay days, people get paid on different days, the mailman, people travel, that's why they built the grace period in. That doesn't necessarily mean that your house is going to be foreclosed upon, but the truth is, they legally could. You are in default if the payment is not received by the 1st.

I explain this to the payers of every single loan that I have, and when they are new to our company, we will send them a late notice on the 2nd, and it'll go out and be postmarked by the 2nd. Even if their payment comes in on the 2nd, they still get a late notice. Now, why do I do that? It establishes the boundaries in the relationship. I made an investment in this note. In order for my investment to work, I have to collect those payments, and I have to collect those payments in a timely fashion, and the timely fashion that I made the investment on had everything to do with what they signed in that note, meaning that the payment is due on the 1st and it's late on the 2nd.

Even if I receive it on the 2nd, and many times things get crossed in the mail, here's what the notice tells them. One, we're paying attention. Two, there's not a lot of grace here. And number three, it lets them know that we want to be the first person on their list of bills that gets paid. I don't want the phone bill, the cable bill, the cell phone bill, the water bill to get paid before the mortgage because if those things get paid before the mortgage, then the mortgage doesn't get paid. If the mortgage gets paid first, then those things will still get paid, because they need those things in order to live.

In other words, when the money dwindles down past the point of what the mortgage payment is, they don't make the mortgage payment, or they postpone it, or they try and get it in on the 15th, or they wait till the 10th or the 15th or the 20th to get it in. Well, now you have somebody that's habitually late in their payment strategy or in their payment history, and now, you're having to wrestle them back to the beginning of the deal that said that this was due on the first, but it's hard to do because they've got limited income. They have a fixed income, and that fixed income only allows for so many things to happen in a given timeframe, so you want to be a constant reminder, and it takes typically about two to five months to really get the point across, but after the point is delivered to the home owner, they will never deviate from that because now that they've created a new habit, a healthy habit, and you've established a boundary with it.

Now, I learned this from a gentleman out of Dallas, Texas who was in the automotive business, and he did "pay here, buy here, pay here" type loans, and he was very successful. He taught me that with seller financing, lower income homeowners tend to live paycheck to paycheck, and in doing that, you have to make sure that you are the first guy to get paid. When he would do auto loans for people, if they didn't pay him when the payment was due, within 24 or 48 hours, he would repo the car. They could come get the car back, but they had to make double or triple payments in order to do it.

He established the boundaries on what the relationship was, and he would tell them up front, "If you don't pay me on the due date, I will come repo your car," and so, they knew that in the back of their minds, so they weren't willing to test the waters. There were very few repos as a whole. There were a few that wanted to test him on it, and he was okay with that, but here's my point in this. This is not about beating people up. This is not about taking advantage of people. This is about adulting. This is about being mature. This is about investment from my part, and homeownership from their part, and that only happens when everybody's working together. If one party is doing whatever they want, and the other party is expecting them to follow the guidelines of what the agreement is, or the legal agreement, then you are going to have chaos, and that chaos leads to business losses.

In 21 years of being in the note space, we have only had eight foreclosures in our performing note side of the business, and it's all because we have established these types of guidelines. It's really nothing more than having a conversation with somebody, and letting them know what you expect of them, and then, letting them also know what they can expect from you, in a lot of different ways.

Now, do we have a heart? Absolutely. If somebody calls me up, and their payment's due on November 1st, and they call me up on October 28th, and say, "Hey, my husband just lost his job. We can't make our payment next month because his paycheck is short and this and this and this. What can we do?" Then we're going to sit down with that homeowner and encourage them to do the number one thing they need to do, go get a job. They need to go get a job because that's what pays all of their bills. Not just me, but all of them, so we will encourage them, and even help them tune up their resume.

We will even forego or postpone a payment or defer a payment to the back of the loan, so that they can focus on getting a job and not making a mortgage payment with us, and that brings a lot of loyalty to the relationship. We really are here to solve problems, but what we are not really interested in is being taken advantage of, and there's a difference. We have had several people call us up in advance because they lost their job and we helped them get back on track. However, we have never done more than defer two payments, because when they are focused in on getting a job versus being worried about making a mortgage payment, guess what happens? They find a job. The beauty of it is that then they are able to get back on their feet, they are able to afford food for their family, electricity for their house, gas for their car, their car payments, all of these other things, and now, we have a client for life, and we have an open line of communication with them to help them out.

We understand in our business that people are going to go through seasons. We understand that people are going to have challenges along the way. Our job is to be an investor. By being an investor in the note space, one of the big things that we do is solve problems. We are here to solve problems because that's what we get paid to do at the end of the day.

In today's note industry, the best thing people can do is to find a servicing company. We have resources for what I would call the top three servicing companies for performing notes, and this is based off of very lengthy track records. These are people that we really like doing business with, and we think most people would like to do business with, and you can get that from our resources page.

I think the industry has become much more streamlined and more user friendly, and I think investors have become much more effective in protecting their investment by helping homeowners out. There are more tools, more resources and more technology. All of that makes the industry more efficient, but it also makes the management and the homeownership more efficient as well.

If you have a servicing company from day one, it is a huge help when and if you ever do want to sell the note, because it's that third-party verification. In other words, if you're selling a six-month-old note, and you have only been servicing for one month, it's not as easy to do due diligence as it is if you already have the servicing company for the entire six months.

It's just one of those things that should happen right at the closing table. Plus, there's no need to re-notify the purchaser because there's no change. In other words, you might keep the same servicing company, and the only change would be who the check is made out to.

When people are doing their deals through title companies, which they should be doing, and getting lenders policies on these loans, if they're connected to what I call one of the top 10 title companies in the country - Fidelity Title, American Title, Chicago Title, and Lawyers Title - you can sign them up for a servicing agreement right there at the closing table. You will have the endorsement of the trusted escrow officer, which are seen as a verification of trust. They will know immediately that their loan is going to be taken care of, and that they're going to get proper credit for all their payments and things of that nature.

I know that a lot of title companies, when they see seller financed deals, will recommend and encourage the parties to engage in that. Some do, some don't, but I think the ones that don't realize very quickly that they made a poor choice because when you go to sell that note, one of the things I'm going to ask for as a note buyer is for them to send me a copy of the pay history. The usual response is, "Well, I just put it in my bank account." Great, now go get me a copy of each deposit slip for every month that this loan has been paying. "Well, I combined it with other checks." Great, go get me that deposit slip. Go, show me that. And now, all of a sudden, they have to spend five, six, seven, eight hours gathering that paperwork to prove that this is a performing loan before it can be sold as a performing loan. Everybody's time is valuable, and they usually learn that mistake pretty quickly.

Every seller we deal with, if they are not using a third-party servicer, is rebuilding the payment history. That's the biggest challenge they have. They can very easily get us a copy of the closing statement, the credit report, the note, the mortgage, the deed, etc. Those are usually readily available.

I would say 90% of the time when people don't use third party servicers, they'll spend anywhere between five to 20 hours gathering even a 12 to 24 month pay history on it, because they have to dig into other files and go back in time to put it together, and it's very cumbersome, and very time consuming.

Because of that, it delays their closing, it delays their cash, it delays their capital. It postpones the sale of the note, because we want to make sure that we're buying a performing note. We want to make sure that we have accurate accounting and history and records and documentation, and at the end of the day, they're the only ones who can supply it, so they have to fit that into their schedule.

What it all boils down to is if you want to put together a high-quality deal, if you want premium pricing, you have to have a premium product, and people that create notes are understanding this. They certainly understand it when they remodel a house, because if they want a premium price out of that remodel, then they've got to have a premium remodel. They have the nice countertops and the cabinets and the flooring and colors and things like that that are trending in today's marketplace. If they don't, that house isn't going to get maximum dollar value. It just never will. It may still sell, but they're going to leave money on the table.

The note business is no different.

Our value comes from documentation. Our value comes from the risk and the return. That's where our value comes from as an investor, and it's up to the person that creates the note to create that as well, at the same time. If they do that, then they're selling the note very streamlined, where they can sell it in a matter of days, versus weeks. Big difference!

Chapter 6

Yields and Returns on Capital

The beauty of our business and the challenge of our business at the same time is the infamous question of "what is your yield?" Or "what kind of return are you looking for?" We get that question on a regular basis from sellers, and we also get that question on a regular basis from investors. How can I make 10% or 12% from the buyer's side and from the seller's side, what kind of yield are you buying at?

My answer to that question is very broad based on my time in the business. It goes like this: we have bought deals at 7% yields, and we have bought deals at 16% yields. I know that's a big, big swing in yield calculations. But here's the reason why. The number one thing that you have to keep in mind when you are buying private notes is that this person or property is not an institutional quality product, which doesn't make it a bad product. It just makes it a higher risk product. Now, higher risk is relative to the overall quality of the deal. What does that mean? Number one, you have to look at it from the banking industry side, which gets their cost capital, which is literally zero. So, if they are lending me money to buy a house and they are lending it to me at three and a half percent, then they are making a three and a half percent spread on that money. But their number one goal, their exit strategy and we've all experienced it, is to loan the money out, create the loan, bundle that loan with a large package of loans, typically ten billion or more, and sell off that entire package in a mortgage backed security marketplace, where they'll get 103 to 108 even as high as 121% of the loan amount.

So, if they lend out $100,000 on a mortgage, they'll bundle that with a portfolio of mortgages somewhere between five to ten billion dollars' worth of product, which ultimately will increase the value to 103% to 108%. Like I said, back in the premium days, it went as high as 121%.

Why do they do that? The masses of product create higher quality bundles which spreads out the risk, which increases the returns on a large-scale loan. That's the institutional mortgage industry. That's the Wall Street mortgage industry. That's the mortgage backed security industry worldwide. That's a model that I can't compete with and I don't know anybody who can.

The reason I share that with you is because people will sell their property to somebody who is not qualified to get a loan from a bank. And yet, that person wants to buy their house and they have decent credit, they have a decent down payment, they have a job, all of those checks are marked but they want a 3% or a 4% interest rate on a 30-year mortgage. And property owners agree to those things. Note holders agree to those types of terms. And they typically agree to them because they're trying to compete with the banks. Well the truth is that they don't have the same structure as an institutional bank.

Why would I tell you that story?

The reason I tell you that story is... don't do that. Do not do those kinds of things if you're creating seller financing. Don't try and compete with a bank that gets their money at zero cost of capital and they lend it out in the multi billions of dollars per week. While you are over here with your one house that you just finished remodeling and now you are trying to compete with Bank of America. If your borrower has the qualifications to go get institutional money, then help them get that institutional money and get your full asking price for your house. I share that story with you to share this story with you. Our industry is a secondary industry. It's a secondary industry for a reason. The core reason is that all of our clients are not institutional quality clients. It doesn't mean they're bad people. It just means that for whatever reason, they don't want to go to the bank and borrow money.

And there is nothing wrong with that. I'm not necessarily excited about banks on a regular basis either. So, when a person comes to us and they want to buy a property, we have to look at it for what it truly is and understand what we are working with as far as borrowers' concern. My advice to people is that they get 10% down, they do 10,20,30- year terms with a 7% to 9% interest rate, no prepayment penalties, no balloons and ideally a 575 or greater credit score. With that, now you put together a note deal that has value in the marketplace. So, when you take it to a note buyer or an investor, who wants to get a 10% return on his or her money, you're taking an 8.5% note to them which is going to minimize your discount tremendously. The other thing that minimizes a person's discount is having a 10-year term versus a 30-year term. Ideally, maybe a 20-year term tends to be the sweet spot in that conversation.

We all have that family relative that we know if we give them money, chances are that we will never see it again. But we often do it to help out family and loved ones and people we care about. The note business is not a charity organization; it's a for profit investing model. So, we have to look at things a little differently. It doesn't mean that we have to be rigid, it just means that we have to understand what we're investing in. Which is the beauty of it, but it can also be the challenge to it as well. If an investor is looking for a return of 10% on the purchase of a note, they are going to be looking at a couple of key indicators. They are going to be looking at the terms. In other words, how long is this mortgage out there? They are also going to be looking at the interest rate of that note or mortgage and the present value of that note, which is its current balance or starting balance. And they are going to be looking at the payment amount and the future value. In that model, let's say somebody creates a note at 20 years with 8.5% interest. They've already checked off that they have decent credit and that they have the down payment that they are comfortable with and the value is there. So, they are looking at a 20-year term, 8.5% interest rate, and the present value being $100,000. On a note of that nature, payment on that amount is going to be $867.82.

To purchase that at a 10% yield, we would purchase that note for $89,927.85. That would be on a 20-year term. If that person had created a note for 360 months, or 30 years, the payment would be $768.91. If we were purchasing it at a 10% yield as well, you'd be paying $87,618.32. So, it's about a $2,000 difference in the overall purchase price of that note. Now the number one thing to always keep in mind that is often forgotten in the business is just because you are getting a 10% yield or 11% or 12%, doesn't necessarily mean that you are making money. I say that because some people have what they call zero cost to capital, meaning if you are pulling money from an IRA or you have money in your savings account or a money market account or out from underneath your mattress, then you have what I call zero cost to capital. So, you would actually be making a 10% return on your money in that model.

If you're borrowing money from a bank line of credit, an equity loan on your house, a credit card, friends or family, there's going to be a cost of capital to that money. Let's say that cost of capital is 5% on the money you are borrowing on an equity loan on your house. Then technically, you are only making about a 5% return on your money because you have the debt service of that loan or that money that you've borrowed. This is much like being a landlord. If you buy the house with institutional money, then every month you collect that rent you have to pay the bank their share. And that's exactly what would happen here. Oftentimes, we forget those aspects to the money.

If you are pulling from your IRA, savings account or checking account, or if you have a couple of family members that are going to contribute and not charge any interest, then that's perfectly okay. That's a zero cost to capital. Here's what becomes tricky. Oftentimes, when the investor is trying to get a 10% return on his or her money, people will bring us notes that are at 3 or 4% interest on a 30-year mortgages or 30-year amortization and they have been seasoned. In other words, payments have been made. And it's working out just fine. And by the way, they always work out just fine when somebody's paying a 3% interest rate because they are not going to walk away from that house if they are only paying 3% interest. Nor are they going to try and refinance that house if that's the current market rate.

I would say about 50% of the time, we see notes that are structured in a fashion that creates a huge discount for the seller in order for an investor to create a modest return on his or her money. Take for instance that same example. If you had $100,000 first lien note on a property and your interest rate on that was, say 4%, over 360 months the payment on that's going to be $477.42. If I were to come along and buy this at a 10% yield, then I would be paying $54,401.86, so it's almost buying it at 50 cents on the dollar. This ties into my earlier chapter about the three different types of sellers. When you end up with sellers who have structured a deal and they premium pricing, or par pricing, that's never going happen here. You end up with a seller who thinks that he's only going to get 20 cents on the dollar or 30 cents on the dollar, he's pretty close to it because of what he did. Or you get a seller who understands what they did and they realize their error but they still need to turn the note so they can get the capital back and go on to the next investment.

This is really, to be quite frank, no different than if you were remodeling homes and you picked the wrong paint color. Do you live with the paint color or do you just bite the bullet and repaint the house knowing that it's going to cost you thousands of dollars to do it and that you are going to sell the house, get your capital out and go to the next deal? That's the same thing that happens with notes.

I love working with note sellers in the beginning stages of the note creation process. I love working with them in that space because it gives me an opportunity to point out the potholes that are on their package so that they can avoid those things and fix them and put together a deal that makes financial sense for both themselves and the property owner. If you think about it, seller financing is really not designed to be a 30-year arrangement or a 20 year. To be honest, no mortgage really is. Institutional or secondary. As a whole, we move around a lot as a society. The average length of a mortgage is 6.9 years. That number comes from is two places:

1. How long a person lives in a house and sells it and moves on.
2. How often a person refinances that house.

We have a tendency to move around and we're movers and shakers as a country. We like to either scale up or scale down or move from one side of the country to the other.

That same thing is true with the seller finance market. If you have somebody at a 7, 8 or 9% interest rate, it's really designed as an incentive for them to clean up whatever they need to in order to go to the bank and get the traditional financing that they need. It's not designed to be a penalty, nor is it designed to be a long-standing relationship. And to be frankly honest with you, rarely is it. The point being, though, as a note investor, we still have to price every note that we purchase based on whatever terms are there. We know as a whole that the majority of them are going to pay off within less than seven years, or refinance. I'm using the word pay off because they are either going to sell the property or refinance the mortgage. This is a positive thing. For them, if they refinance it, it saves them money. If they sell the property, hopefully they make money through equity on the sale of the house.

So keep in mind, when we are working with note sellers, and investors, what are their costs to capital. If it's a zero cost to capital, it's very easy to deal with. If there's a cost to capital, maybe 5%, then we need to understand that we are only really making a 5% return on that investment. Which, to be truthful, is still a lot better than the stock market or CD's or money market accounts or any of those other things that we often compare it to.

Partial Notes

During a typical investment, we designed a tool that we use internally on a regular basis. It's an investment calculator that we use to calculate all the notes that we purchase. The beautiful thing is it only requires about three or four more pieces of information. One requires the present value of the note, or the starting balance of the note, also known as the starting balance, present value, your interest and then the term of the note in months. We do it in months, not in years because we found that a lot of times amortization schedules are not 240 months or 20 years, it's 243 months. Also, it's based on how people put them together. Then there are balloon payments and payments made; how many payments have they currently made up to date. What we are able to do is to go in there and put in whatever our desired yield is based on whatever the cost of capital is at that moment in that time. Whether we are zero cost to capital because I have money to send out of my IRA, or I have a cost to capital that I'm going pull from a line of credit or I have some business partners or investors, wherever we're going to pull that capital from will determine our yield as a whole.

We are plugging in the note amount, the interest rate, the terms of months, the balloon, if there is one. If there isn't, it's simply number of payments made in months and then our desired yield. With that it spits out what we call a net purchase price. A net purchase price is our "all in" price, sometimes known as a retail purchase price. The difference in retail versus wholesale in our business is simply explained this way. If I'm buying it retail, that means this is my all-in number and we pay the closing costs for the note seller. That means we have to buy the title, appraisals, etc.

When we use this investment calculator, the first thing that we're basing our original offer off is information that the seller has given us, which I would say most cases, if not all cases, sound a lot like this: this guy's an awesome homeowner, he's never missed a payment with us, he takes amazing care of the house, it's put in a fashion where you're excited to purchase it. Not saying that it changes, but the point being is that they're going to make it sound as good as humanly possible because they want the most amount of money possible with a note.

When we figure out our yield, or we go in there and we price it out, we always want to go in it with the best possible attitude and the desire to purchase it. When we want to purchase notes, the goal is not to turn down notes. The goal is to purchase notes and invest in those. So, we'll figure out what that yield is based on what I call a happy medium. Not a 7% yield, but also not a 16% yield. I like being in that 10% yield range, which is a lot like being a fisherman, where you cast out a really big net. You're not going to catch all the fish, but you're going to catch a good portion of the fish. Yes, you could have a bigger net, but you could also have a smaller net as well. That's the way we approach the business, knowing that the original quotes are always going to be subject to due diligence and credit review.

With our software, we can also go in there and look at it from a partial note purchase. Partial notes are the exciting aspect to our business. When you look at a partial or buy a note on a partial, what you're doing is exactly what it stands for - partial. You're buying a portion of the note. They don't need to sell their entire $100,000 note. They just need to sell $20,000 because their kid starts college in 30 days and they have to pay for college tuition. So, they just need to sell $20,000 of it.

The Power of Paper

You can easily come in there and buy something along those lines. Take a $100,000 note, that would be a million ... and that's at 8.5% rate on 360-month terms and you want to buy it at 10% yield to get them $20,000. You would approximately buy 30-months-worth of payments and that would net them $20,335. Now if you figure closing costs in there, you may want to buy 31 or 32 payments, or the seller can pay closing costs. Basically, what we would be doing is saying, "Okay Mister Seller, you've got a 360 month note and you have paid nine payments on it. You've got 351 payments left. We're going buy the next 30 payments and we're going to collect the next 30 payments. After we receive the 30th payment, we are going to assign the note back to you and you will go on collecting the rest of them."

What often happens is when they get to about the 20-payment mark, they need more money. It kind of works like an annuity for them. So, they will come back and say, "Can you buy another 30 payments," or another 40 payments or another 50 payments, whatever they're capital needs are. We can re-visit the file, because we have it. We have had it for 20 months and we're comfortable with it. All the payments are on time and the borrower's smooth sailing. And we can in turn look at it very quickly, make them an offer for an additional 40 payments or 50 payments or 100 payments, whatever meets their monetary needs.

With that, we do a couple of due diligence checks and balances, write them a check, give them a contract extending out the number of payments that we are purchasing and they in turn get money and we just extend from 30 to 70 payments because we bought an extra 40 payments on the deal. It works a lot like an annuity for them because when we purchase a partial, we take the full assignment of that partial and we have total control of it until we receive all 30 payments, as in the original example.

The servicing entity that services the loan for us collects the payments and keeps everybody up to date on the numbers and the year-end filings and all of those other aspects to it. Partials are very, very popular and I highly recommend partials in this business because it achieves the goal for the seller. Most sellers don't need $90,000 of their $100,000. That's not really what they're looking for. What they're looking for is a small amount of money that is directly proportionate to whatever challenge they have, aka, sending their kid to college could be a monetary challenge. You need to pay for those kinds of things. It could even be a health issue. It could be they have an opportunity to start a new business and they may not need all that money, but they don't know any other way to sell it. So, educating them on, "Yes. We can purchase it as a full and it would be X dollars, or purchasing it on a partial of 30 payments would be $20,335. Which would suit your needs the best?" In other words, speaking to their "why" on why they are selling helps them to understand the options that they have.

Now I want to put this little caution aspect to doing partials. Partials only work if there's little to no debt on the property. Using this example of $100,000 at 8.5% interest on 360-month terms, nine payments being made, and the seller needs $20,000 to send his son to college. Well, let's say they've got a $25,000 loan on the property. Meaning, they bought the house and they lived it in for 10 years. Then they moved into a bigger house and they sold this house with seller financing. We need to pay off that $25,000 loan to whomever it's to. Not a big deal. All we need to do here is to go in and instead of buying 30 payments, we're probably going to need to buy 82 more. Now we are investing $45,000 at the closing and the $45,000 is going to be about 82 payments. So, $25,000 is going to go to the underlying lien or the bank that has the lien against the property, and then $20,547 is going to go the note holder. Oftentimes this is referred to as a wrap in our industry. And we do wraps on a regular basis. We will get more into wraps in a later chapter as a whole. But that's the key ingredient into making partials work. Partials work amazingly well for people that have free and clear properties or very little debt against their properties. People that are highly leveraged, or have a lot of liens against their property and they're trying to sell it, the only way that I've seen that works consistently in the business is to sell the entire thing, pay off the underlying liens and whatever is left over, the note holder gets at that point in time.

The Power of Paper

Chapter 7

Passive Investors

Even though we are on the leading edge of alternative investments, when push comes to shove, given the stability of the return and the risk reward ratio, notes are still the very best place for you to have your own money, and therefore it's the best place for our investors to have their own money.

Notes are one of those things where to me, I look at it as being a success. Meaning that once you purchased one, you add it to your portfolio, and you start growing your portfolio; you're guaranteed that return or that yield is 8,9, 10, 12, 15%, for the next 30 years. Like the stock market, a 401K or any kind of a fund management perspective, they will count that year where they received 15% returns. If you look at it over the life cycle of the fund, that only happened two out of the last 10 years. They were excited about it, it was a great year and they did hit some home runs, and use that byproduct of good management and good timing.

You can't invest based on just that one or two-year return, whereas notes bring that consistent return. If you buy that at a 12% yield, then that's 12% for the next year. Let's say there was 27 years left on the mortgage that you bought - 27 years, 12%. That's a phenomenal model. Obviously if they pay off early, your yield actually goes up. That's even more exciting. When they pay off early, most people will either sell or refinance their house, which results in you being paid your complete unpaid principle balance. That's a good thing!

When I got into the note business, the thing that attracted me to it first and foremost was the fact that you could put your money to work, but you didn't have to work your money. That eulogy of, hey how'd your money work for you, versus you working for it, really applied in the note space above and beyond anything else I could find at the time. That theory is still true today, and if you look at why the wealthy and the super wealthy invest in notes and mortgages, it's because they understand 1. the art of compound interest, and 2. they understand that their money is constantly working for them, that 24/7 model that is talked about on a regular basis at real estate investment clubs around the country.

The truth to it is two-fold. One, you have to have the money to invest in the notes, but keep in mind notes come in all different sizes. I've seen them at $10,000 and I've seen them at $10,000,000. As matter of fact, we had the opportunity back in '06 to buy the loan on Michael Jackson's Never, Never Land ranch in California. It was brought to us by a private group that owned it and wanted to sell it. We ended up passing on it, but it was a $32,000,000 note that they wanted to sell on his house. We have seen the range in which notes exist, and you get into even second lien notes, which get a little smaller. For those investors that are just starting out, that's a great place to get your feet wet. Buy either a second lien, or ideally a first lien for $10-20,000, put that in your portfolio and allow that to work for you.

Now, the simple truth and what a lot of the gurus won't tell you is that it takes money to be in the note business. You have to have money from your own pocket, meaning your 401Ks, IRAs, your stocks, dividends, cash, savings, bonds, mutual funds, mattress, where your money's at. You have to have that money to invest, or you have to have access to capital or money in the form of JV Partnerships, friends and family, business lines of credit, equity lines of credit on properties, things of that nature, where you can leverage that money into a return as well.

At the end of the day, what's so attractive about notes and mortgages is just the fact that once the deal is done, and it's what they call booked into your servicing firms files, now it's just a matter of collecting money on a very passive format. Now, there's a secret to this whole thing, and it really depends on the goal of the investor. It could go one of two ways. You can collect that money, and you can bank it and invest in another note down the road. You can collect it and allow it to grow, and then reinvest it, which is the ideal model, because especially if you're at a time in your life where you don't necessarily need the cash, you can leverage the cash into other notes and increase your cash flow. That would be plan number one.

Plan number two is people receive that money, they spend the money, and then they wait for the next month's check to come along. The good and bad in that is two-fold. One is, if you have just a single note deal, and you're collecting $400 a month off of it, even though it's an amazing return, if you keep spending that $400 a month every month, then ultimately, you're not going to receive the full value. You're not going to realize and experience the full amount of that money because it taps into what I call investors amnesia. Investors amnesia is where you take the money you're earning off your investments, and you're spending it on things that don't increase in value.

You're eating the principle, you're eating the interest, and therefore come the end of the year, you're not going to realize the full value. You're going to see it, because it's going to show up on your tax return in the form of interest earned, but you're ultimately not going to realize it or get the full value of it, because it's interest spent as well. I like to tie that into January of every year. Employed Americans get a W2, and in January of every year they look at that and go, "where'd all the money go," because of the lack of money in savings and other things. They have to sit down and scratch their head to figure out where all the money went. The truth is, they spent it. They were earning it and spending it on daily activities.

You have to be very disciplined in that space. The ideal model for the passive income is to invest in the notes, to board the notes with a servicing company, and have the servicing company put the money into a money market account, savings account or a checking account that for all intents and purposes is either one, an emergency fund, or is allowed to accumulate until you find your next deal, and not to use it on daily expenses. That way the money materializes in its entirety, grows like you wanted it to, and you can accomplish the goal as you laid out. If you have the discipline and can apply that discipline to it, then whoever that investor is will ultimately receive the maximum value out of that investment - over and above just spending it each and every month that they get that check.

A lot of times when people create notes, it kind of falls into that same category. They go to sell a property, they carry back the note, they think it's pretty amazing, and it is. When you look at the numbers, it is very amazing. There is a difference between the numbers and reality in everybody's world. They are looking at numbers like wow, this is a great return, based on their investment in the property and whatever they have invested overall, what they sold it for and now they've got this note. When it really breaks down to the fact that they are receiving a $600 or $700 a month payment, and in the beginning, it sounds enlightening. What they realize is two years down the road, or two months, or six months, whatever it may be, when you only have one note deal, now all of a sudden, it's like, do I want $600 a month, or do I want $50,000 cash. Most passive investors or note holders will cash out because they want that $50,000 cash versus that $600 a month.

The wise thing about that is if they have a place that they can go and use that 50 grand to reinvest into another property, or another opportunity, then that's a wonderful idea, especially if it's exponentially growing for them. It's not a wonderful idea if their goal is just to cash out and go buy a fifth wheel trailer to park in their backyard and use once or twice a month during the summer. That's not a wise idea. It really depends upon what the goal and objective is with that particular investor, or that particular note holder on the passive side.

The great thing about being a passive investor with notes is that not only can you use cash on hand to invest in notes, but nowadays you can get into using Roth money or IRA money to get into tax deferments.

What I love about the IRA, over and above just the tax benefits to it, is it's almost like your money is on lockdown, and that's a good thing for a lot of people, myself included. There are parts of my life where I'm more disciplined than others, and I think that runs for everybody worldwide, whether you're an American or not. The point being is that when you have excess money, you pull from a retirement account and you invest it in a note. That money's going right back into that account for you. Not only are you receiving the tax benefits of that investment, but also now you've got your hands in lockdown because you can't get that money.

If you're a shopaholic, for example, and that $600 a month payment is not overly exciting to you, you're just spending it anyways. A much better model to use would be to apply it to your investing model, because now you're actually getting to your goal. That allows your money to accumulate into an account that has tax benefits on an annualized basis, as well as retirement basis, and ultimately allows your money to grow. If you want to sell the note, you can certainly sell the note as well. It allows you to do those kinds of things. If you want to buy more notes, you can obviously buy more notes with that accumulated money that's come into that account for you, so you can keep leveraging up.

My encouragement for people that are interested in the note space is really simple: whenever you want to invest, make sure that it's not your entire portfolio, but it's only a percentage of your portfolio. If you say,

The Power of Paper

"Well, I've got 50 grand I want to invest," or, "I've got a retirement account I want to use that money with," then that's wonderful. In other words, learn the business. Learn if it's for you, learn if it's working for you. Mathematically, it works for everybody. It may not necessarily work for everyone because it moves too slow, or it doesn't accumulate fast enough, or the numbers don't grow exponentially on a 30-day period. My experience with those types of investors is that they need something a lot more aggressive in a return type model, versus something like notes, which are just slow and steady.

The 2017 Roth IRA contributions right now are $5,500. Now, in order to have a Roth, you have to have an income limit of $186,000, which is a good thing because obviously that gives a lot of people the opportunity to invest. When you're married and filing jointly, your income limit can be anywhere from $186,000 to $195,000, but here's the great part. They're beginning to phase out your contribution limits. You have to meet with a custodian and find out exactly what the save schedule is over the next several years that will allow them to contribute more to it.

The thing that people have to understand about limits is that you can put above the $5,500 as currently stated as of this writing, but you're going to pay a penalty on it. That penalty is very small, usually around 3% or less. The question then becomes as an investor, what is my upside value if I put more money in here than what they will allow you to, and I pay the penalty. Can I gain that back in the purchase of this note? That's a way of contributing more, paying a penalty, but getting your money working for you at a much quicker pace. This becomes a numbers thing, especially if you have a note deal and it's a 14% yield. If you pay a 3% penalty on the money, you're still at an 11% yield. That's a good thing.

It's a one-time penalty. The other thing that you can do with the Roth's and retirement accounts is you can JV on deals. Let's say you've been putting $5,500 in every year, and you accumulated $20,000, but all of a sudden, a note deal comes along, and there's an opportunity to invest as partial owner in that note deal. If you feel more comfortable just owning it all yourself, find a note deal that fits your buying parameters.

A lot of times people say, "How do I find a $20,000 note deal? That's all I've got." Here's a little secret - those $20,000 note deals are not found everywhere. You can find them in Scottsdale, Arizona, but you can't find them in Yuma, Arizona. You can find them in Tucson, Arizona or Hildebrand, Arizona. In other words, what I'm saying is, you go to these lower price point communities, or areas of the country where home pricing is 30, 40, $50,000, whatever it may be, and you can find a note that you can buy for 20, $25,000.

If you go in and you buy a partial, and the seller needs $20,000, and you buy the 30 payments for $20,000 and those payments are going into your IRA, guess what? You're still under that 6.9-year average. Rather than putting money out for 30 years, you're only putting money out for 30 months, and you're going to get the same return but you're going to have less capital involved and ultimately, you're going to gain that return back into your IRA. If they come along at the 24th month and say, "I need another 20 grand," you are going to have that 20 grand in your IRA, or your retirement account, that you can ultimately apply to the next investment.

Partials are a great place to start as well. You basically have a couple choices. You can do partials with small amounts of money, you can do smaller balanced loans with smaller amounts of money, or you can do syndicates and JVs with smaller amounts of money. The number one goal for anybody starting out would be to find what their comfort level is, to find out where they feel the most secure with a first-time investment, and to seek out that level of investment. In other words, when my parents invested their money, we didn't do anything crazy with it. Their deals are very straight forward, very simple, very plain 30- year terms, 9% interest rate, decent credit, good money down, and equity into property. That's what they like. There are deals out there that are regularly available, considering we're dealing in a $2,000,000,000,000 marketplace. There's plenty of opportunity for people to find deals that match what their investing criteria is.

Chapter 8

Time Value of Money

The driving force behind seller financing is a two-fold model. Number one is it gives the property owner an opportunity to sell their property, where in a lot of cases, they couldn't have sold it, either due to property type or location, and even so much as the qualifications of the buyer. Seller financing gives the property owner the opportunity or the tools and resources to make that happen, and to bring that to completion or fruition. What most property sellers don't understand is that when they do this, there is a series of steps they need to go through in order to create a high-quality note, just like there's a series of steps that you need to go through to create a high-quality product of any kind, whether that's a car, a house, a boat, a plane.

You always want the best or the highest quality possible. The reason most people don't know these things is because they don't take the time to really understand them. More importantly, the key driving force behind all of this is what we call time value of money. The time value of money principle centers around the money being worth more today than it will be in the future. This model's been proven to be 100% accurate, throughout our lives, based on two key aspects: 1. the dollar continues to decline in value, and 2. our costs continue to go up, day in and day out, meaning our cost of capital, and what people can use that money for. A simple way to look at it is if you have a $100,000 note, and you could receive $75,000 for that today, what could you actually do with that $75,000 that would far exceed the $25,000 discount, or the 25% discount that you might take on that. The greatest way to look at it is if you're looking at the face value of that note, that $100,000, and you're receiving a $1,000 a month payment, do you want to consider receiving the $1000 a month payment, or would you prefer, say, $75,000 lump sum cash? What can you do more with in that scenario? And most people have opportunities that they could use the $75,000 for, versus the $1,000 a month cash flow.

That is the simplicity behind time value of money. Now, to make sure that time value of money works in your favor when you sell a note, use that money as an investment tool to go into another financial opportunity of greater proportion. Meaning that if your model was to fix and flip homes, you were better off using that lump sum of cash going into buying another house or a couple more properties, or to finish up a larger property, or a larger project that gives the greater returns.

What you don't want to be doing is using that money to go out and buy something that is a depreciating asset like a boat or a car or something along those lines. That in itself is not a wise move, when it comes down to using that lump sum of cash intelligently. The majority of the sellers that we work with have a game plan for using that money, and they already have an idea of what they want to use the money for. In most cases it is used for things like offsetting medical costs, sending children to college, buying more properties, paying off high interest debt, or investing in opportunities that will bring them a much greater return over the life of the investment like the paying off their own personal mortgage.

Things like that apply to the season of life that the person is in. We deal with clients that are early 30s all the way up to early 70s, and what I've learned is during the spectrum of ages, people have different needs, different desires, different goals and different directions that they want to go in life. A 30-year-old might use that money to go out and buy more properties and continue building their portfolio, whereas somebody in their early 60s might find better value paying off medical costs or paying off their mortgage. It's a personal decision.

You can also structure the numbers in a lot of different ways in order to produce a type of outcome. You hear some people say, "Well, no. Keep the cash flow forever, to create cash flow. Cash flow is king," and although that principle is a great principle, people have to make a decision on their own, depending upon where they are at in their own season of life, and whether or not cash flow is more important than a lump sum of money.

Having a $1,000 cash flow when you are burdened with $50,000 in debt is not necessarily a great trade-off for somebody who's in their early 60s; they could relinquish that debt or pay it off and be debt free. We are a big fan of helping people become debt free, simply because it eases the burden of living, so they are not having to go out there to earn that money or rely on that money all the time, so time value of money is a really simple principle.

Money is worth more today than it will be in the future, and that's been proven throughout the history of our country, just simply due to the declining value of the dollar today, versus what it used to be. Not to mention that most of the mortgages that we see or notes that we see are typically 20+ years in length, which means that we're having to wait. In the example, $75,000 on a $100,000 note, that person gets that $75,000 cash today. We're unfortunately waiting the next 30 years to capture that $25,000 discount, plus our interest, plus, plus, plus.

So, at the end of the day, it gives that person who has the note a lot more freedom to choose what the next direction is going to be, either in their personal life, their business life, spiritual life, whatever that may be on how they see a better fit for the use of that money moving forward.

Some of the most interesting questions that we get with sellers that create notes, or people that have ideas about real estate notes are number one, "if I charge a high interest rate, am I going to get a premium price paid for my note?" Although there was some truth to that 20 years ago, that truth is no longer valid in today's market and/or economy. They are charging high interest rates, meaning the mid-teens and higher. What we have learned throughout history is that if people cannot afford the payment, they won't make the payment, and no matter what the yield might calculate to be on the purchase of that note, when people stop making payments on that mortgage, that yield goes to zero. So, at the end of the day, note buyers shy away from high interest notes, primarily because we learned over the course of the history of our industry that they unfortunately will go into default at some point in time, usually sooner versus later. That's number one.

Number two is, "I can just sell my house to anybody. And I don't need to run their credit." I see these Bandit signs throughout my hometown here in Phoenix, Arizona, saying, "No bank qualifying. No credit check," and those types of signs are a recipe for disaster when it comes to seller financing in our space. Why are they a recipe for disaster? Well, it's simple. You lose the opportunity to learn something about another person, especially when you are extending them a line of credit, which is what you're doing. You're lending them money through seller financing, so you need to find out those things about them at the front side of the relationship.

The time to run their credit is today, to find out if they have the ability to pay you, based on how they are paying other people. The biggest mistake that I see in the space is that people don't run a buyer's credit, and unfortunately are shocked when they find out that the property buyer has a 520-credit score and they haven't paid anybody in the last two years.

Now, I want to be really sensitive here.

I understand that everybody goes through seasons. I've been through seasons of life myself. I have a tremendous respect for people that are going through different seasons in life. My advice to people that are going through tough times is to try to get things cleaned up so that they are reflective of where you are at today versus where you were two years ago or three years ago. If you have gone through seasons that have cost you credit cards or poor credit standings, get those things cleaned up before you go out and purchase another house.

Note property sellers who are creating seller financing need to be pulling credit on their home buyers, and they need to be pulling credit on their home buyers so that they understand that the overall quality of that buyer is a high-quality buyer that's going to continue to have the ability to make payments. We base those types of decisions off of their actions, not off of what they tell us. Their actions appear in the credit report, meaning that if they are not paying anybody, then there's a strong probability that they're not going to pay on this note for very long. We have seen that over and over and over again with people.

It's not that they are doing anything right or wrong. It's just that they are not out of that season of life that they are working through, and you don't need to be a part of it until they are completed. The thing that scares me the most about this particular behavior is that people will go out and hand over the keys to a $100,000 asset and not even take the time to find out the credit worthiness of the home buyer. Turning the keys over in that fashion in a legal binding contract is very hard to unravel. Not to mention, it will unfortunately be very costly in the end, when and if that buyer starts to default on that mortgage.

That default will cost everybody money, but more importantly, when they go to sell that note, as a note buyer, we're going to pull credit on that buyer, and when we pull credit, and we discover that they have a 520 credit score and they haven't paid anybody for several years, and they are caught up in collections and judgment issues, we are not going to want that in our portfolio, or we are going to purchase it at a much steeper discount in order to put it in our portfolio.

That is very big eye-opening aspect to what is typically taught in the marketplace. What's typically taught in the marketplace is to find a buyer and get money down. If they default, you can foreclose, and you get their down payment money. Well, majority of the time, the down payment money won't even handle the foreclosure process and/or the foreclosure cost, or the legal cost associated with removing them from the property. Not to mention the time and the lost opportunity. When you add all that together, it far exceeds, in most cases, the amount of money that somebody's received as a down payment.

So, it's a very risky move to build a business model around that type of a scenario, yet I see that it's being taught in the educational market space on a regular basis. The reality of that is when you do that, and you sell a property without running a person's credit, and you carry back the paper on it, when you go to sell that paper, it has very little value in the marketplace, and that in itself is going to be very costly. But that one decision early on in the process is typically not realized until a period of three, four, five, six months down the road.

You can't turn back the hands of time when you do that. You need to run credit on the borrowers. You need to find out where they are currently at financially as well as what they have been paying on, what they haven't been paying on, so you can make a much better decision, and also have the ability to guide them, if need be.

The next thing that I want to talk about here is down payment. "Hey, I don't need any money down. I heard about no money down loans. I heard about no money down seller financing, and that's the model I want to go with." Although I understand that may be the model you want to go with, there is an important reason for having people put down at least 5% -10% on a seller financed transaction; it is so they have a vested interest in the deal.

There's a psychology behind this, and those of us that do this every day understand the psychology. If they don't have anything invested in it, they are not going to take care of it. Not only are they not going to take care of the property, they are also not going to take care of making sure the payments are on time, because they don't have any reason to care. In other words, if I know that I can skip my payment, and I've got you locked into a contract and it's going to take you six months to get me out of this contract, and you are not even reporting it on my credit in the first place, then I don't care, as a home buyer, because I don't have anything to lose. This is why you should run their credit, and why they should have money down.

If I have money down, meaning I've put down 10% or say, $10,000 and on a $100,000 home purchase, now I've got a completely different attitude about our agreement. The number one attitude I have about it, is, hey, I have money invested in this house. I'm going to take care of it. Number two, I have got money invested in this house. I don't want to lose my hard-earned money, so I want to make sure my payments are on time, and I'm going to make sure that I make them every month. No matter what I have to do, I am going to make sure that that happens. That in itself is a huge, huge part of anybody's psychology. Here's a story I like to use: think about that very first bike that you got for Christmas or for a birthday. Now think about it sitting on the side of the house with a flat tire and left out in the rain and the sun and the snow. It didn't really get well taken care of! Now think about the first bike *you* had to buy as a kid. That bike was garage kept, and if it got a flat tire, it was fixed very quickly, and it was always tuned up and the chain was oiled, etc.

In other words, psychologically speaking, if I have something invested, then I have something to lose, and I don't want to lose that, and most people don't want to lose anything, yet alone, their hard-earned money. So, you want to make sure that they have ideally 10% or greater invested. I understand that can be a little difficult on some of the bigger deals out there, but we want to focus on making sure they have got substantial skin in the game that makes them think twice about skipping your payment, or not taking care of that house or property, as well as not skipping the insurance payment or the taxes. All of that is part of it.

The next one would be making sure they have the ability to pay, no matter what. One of the things that's important about lending somebody money is that they are going to pay you back. At some level, we've all lent people money. Maybe not under the structure of seller financing, but the structure of a gentleman's agreement, or a promise to pay type agreement, and when we've gotten that money back, it built our relationship and our trust. If we didn't get the money back, it broke down our relationship and our trust.

In the seller financing model, the thing to remember is that you are giving that person a loan; you are extending credit to that person, so you need to make sure that that person has the ability to repay. I've felt this way for 21 years. Prior to Dodd-Frank, we would always income qualify our buyers to make sure that our buyers had the ability to pay us back.

We are extending or purchasing a loan, or a note, so we want to make sure that that's going to happen because that is our recovery model. So, if I give somebody $75,000 for a $100,000 note, I want to make sure that it gets repaid, based on the terms of the agreement. It's important for the person who's creating the note to do the same thing - to make sure that the home buyer, whoever they may be, whether it's a single person or a couple, has the ability to make that payment in a timely fashion.

Tips of the Trade

Majority of the time, people make payments that are due on the first of the month. The first tip would be to find out how that person makes their living, and if they get paid on the 10th and 20th of the month. In this scenario, it would be better to set up their monthly payment on the 12th of the month, because they will be on time paying right after they receive their paycheck. That gives them and you the structure for success. In other words, you are working with them, instead of against them. If they are supposed to make the payment the first of the month, but they are not paying you till the 15th because they are getting paid on the 10th, then they are going to be late. They are going to be hit with late fees, and it's going to set a tone that is going to create an undertone to the relationship. So, set them up with payments dates that work with their pay schedule.

Make sure that they have a substantial amount of money to live on, meaning about 37% - 40% debt-to-income. Pull their credit report, calculate the debt to income calculation, so that they are set up to win.

Here's the key: If you are going to seller finance an individual or a couple, set the terms of the agreement so that it is successful for not only them, meaning it doesn't burden them with unnecessary debt or a pay schedule that they are not able to adhere to, and set yourself up for success so that come the 10th of the month, or the 12th of the month, that you are receiving your payments on time. That way, the relationship is built on a healthy foundation, versus one that's built off of an industry standard, or an industry model that's inconsistent to that relationship.

If you are setting it up for the first of the month, and they don't get paid until the 10th, you are going to be frustrated, as a note holder, because you are always getting your payments late, and that's no fun. At the end of the day, seller financing should be designed as a passive investment for either the person that's creating it, or for the investor buying it.

The Power of Paper

The last but not least tip is selling the property based on its true value, and the guide, here, and it's one that I've recommended for years, is that people take the time to go out and get an accurate appraisal on the property before they list it for sale. Now, I say that for a couple of reasons: 1. I know that people put a lot of hard work in cleaning up homes and properties and remodeling them and I want to make sure that those people get 100% of the full value of the effort that they put into that property.

2. Trying to be an expert in the area of appraising homes is not the strength of most people. So, hiring an expert that has gone through and is a licensed appraiser, having him or her come in and do a full appraisal on the property, especially if you add in square footage, and to capture the full value of a person's efforts on that property when it comes to remodeling, gives them the solid foundation to sell the property. So, if the property value is $100,000, and your guessing it's $120,000 and you're going to sell it for $120,000 even though the real value is $100,000, you are going to find out when you go to sell that the note is going to come in at a lower price point than you might expect. Somebody's going to come along, get an appraisal on the property, and unfortunately, they are going to see that this property's only worth $100,000, even though you sold it for $120,000. In that scenario, the truth is, we're going to base the purchase price off of the lower of the two. The seasoned investors of the industry have learned that that home owner is most likely going to go into default. They will find out that they have overpaid for that property, so to set a level playing field in the relationship, you want to make sure that you have established the value prior to listing the property for sale. Or, if you find out the real value of the property is $100,000, and you sold it for $110,000, make the appropriate adjustments on that contract so that it's reflected accordingly.

That way, you build trust in your buyer, you build trust in your relationship, and you're putting together a quality deal that the marketplace wants to purchase. If you choose to sell the property for $120,000, when it's worth $100,000, you are going to be shocked at the low prices that you are going to receive on that note at the end of the day. It's not worth what you think it is.

You don't attract the top of the barrel. You tend to attract the worst of the worst, and you end up inheriting built-in problems, and that's not the goal of the note buyer, and it shouldn't be the goal of the property seller. The writing of this book, and the idea behind this book is really to shed light and help both parties in the transaction to put together quality financial transactions. You don't want to be attracting buyers that are going to create problems for the note holder, whether that's the original person, or it's the future note buyer that may come along and purchase the note.

The beauty of the industry is that we have the opportunity to choose who to sell houses to, based on some criteria that I just mentioned: client worthiness, down payment and income ability. Those are very, very useful tools in the marketplace to find quality buyers. Quality buyers with quality homes equal quality transactions, and as long as note sellers, or people who are using seller financing follow that methodology, they will continue to create quality deals that they can take to the marketplace and use time value of money to accelerate and grow their business, versus having their money locked up for extended periods of time that fall outside of their business model.

A lot of times, I hear people and I have talked to people who say, "Well, I sold the house because this person goes to my church, or this person is my son's soccer coach, or this person is this and this person is that." I'm a big proponent of helping people. However, we still have to go through the same process when we are helping somebody who's a friend as we would if we were helping somebody who is a stranger, and that way, we set up quality deals. I've said this before: some people are not necessarily good candidates for the seller financing model because they are in a season of life that they are not quite finished with, and they need to spend a little more time there. Those people might be better suited as a tenant for a rental property than they are as a home buyer for a lot of different reasons.

The thing to always remember, and they do it in the rental industry, nationwide, is every time they rent an apartment or a house, and anybody who's a landlord reading this will be shaking their head up and down, they always pull that tenant's credit, and they always want to know that tenant has a job. Yet, here they are, just renting the house or apartment to that person. Most of the landlord laws allow them to evict a tenant in 30 days or less, nationwide, whereas the foreclosure laws are typically 90 days or more, nationwide. If they have to go through that credit check and income verification background to just rent an apartment or a house for a period of time, why wouldn't they have to go through that same thing, if not more, if they were actually investing or purchasing their own house?

Another thing that you really need to be clear about is up until the day of closing, all those financial problems belong to the buyer, but after the closing, the note holder inherits all of those financial problems, and they become a party to this person's season of life, if you will. Once that closing takes place, now they are married to that person for an indefinite period of time, and the idea that that relationship goes well, the truth is, sometimes it doesn't.

We have to, as investors, be responsible for making sure that the people that we are doing business with are people who are in a season of life that have the ability to maintain and uphold their end of the agreement, at the end of the day. If they don't, those problems that you saw on the front side will manifest themselves on the back side of that relationship.

If you end up in the worst-case scenario, which is to foreclose on the property, the cost of the foreclosure is not just the lost revenue from each month's payment. You also have insurance, the legal cost of foreclosure filing, the attorney cost for representation. You also have property taxes that need to be kept up.

Safeguards

To wrap up this chapter, there are a couple of simple things that people can do when they carry back the note. They have gone through the process of finding out who this person is, and they have set terms. One of the best recommendations I can give anybody out there who is doing seller financing is that once the loan is created is to place it with a servicing company and allow that servicing company to collect the payments for them. I understand it's an additional cost of anywhere between $6 to $15 a month to do that, but the value that it brings is tremendous, in the sense that that servicing company will keep you updated on the taxes being paid in a timely fashion. They will issue the year-end interest statements to both the note holder and the property buyer.

They will also stay on top of the homeowner's insurance based on its annual renewal or monthly payments and manage the entire process for the note holder. The beautiful side of that is that when a note holder goes to sell a note, it's very simple for them to contact their servicing company and ask them to produce the payment history. Because of technology, they can go into a personal portal on the servicer's website, and just print out the pay history. That gives us as a note buyer tremendous confidence that the payments that have been received on that note have been received according to the ledgers that are given to us. The taxes are up to date, the insurance has been kept up to date, and it builds tremendous confidence in what they call a "checks and balance" system for all the party's involved.

The homeowner is getting their payments applied correctly, the homeowner is getting their year-end tax statement, which is a tremendous value for them. Come tax season, it is one of the biggest line item deductions that homeowners get to put on their taxes. It also gives the investor or the note holder their tax statement as well, so they can put that in their taxes and have an accurate account of interest income received from that note. It keeps the books in line, and it becomes a very turn-key model for the note holder. That one value in itself of paying an extra $6 to $15 plays into it.

Sometimes, people will get a little out of sorts and don't want to spend the $10 a month. Well, there are two ways to handle it. One, as a note holder, you can pay the $10 out of your proceeds, or number two, you can build that cost into the note, per month, over and above the payment amount that the homeowner pays. So, if it's $10 a month, you would just an additional $10 to every month's payment. That would go to the servicing company, and then, they would still net out the same amount of money. But even if you have to pay it out of your own pocket, paying that $10 a month, as an example, is $120 a year, which basically buys dinner for a couple on a date night.

But more importantly, it keeps your books in order.

It gives proper credit where credit is due, both to the buyer and the note holder, and it ends up creating a very simple year-end accounting for both the buyer and the seller. So, that in itself, I would highly recommend as another tip for creating a high-quality note structure or note environment.

The Power of Paper

When we see that aspect of a note sellers model, it brings a tremendous relief to us as note buyers that they put together a deal, and they put together key components that created a quality deal for everybody involved.

The Power of Paper

Chapter 9

Property Titles

There's a multitude of things that will come up in due diligence or the early stages of a note purchase. One of the things to identify early on is what type of title you have on the property. You have your fee simple, which is probably your most common type of title on a property. Then you have lease hold, which is a different type of title to the property. A lease hold property is a title where you own the building, but you don't own the ground. That was very common back in the early years in the formation and establishment of the US, and it continued on until the early '70s, at which point in time laws were enacted where you could convert the lease hold into a fee simple by simply buying out the lease.

In layman's terms, if you lease a piece of property for X number of years and you pay X dollars, you can purchase it if you choose to, or you can just rent it. In this case, lease hold is renting the dirt or the piece of land that the house sits on. Areas of the country that are very popular and common for this are places like Washington, DC, Baltimore, Virginia, Philadelphia, parts of New York, Hawaii, Chicago and Boston, just to name a few.

The great part about lease hold in today's day and age is that it is very easy to convert it from lease hold to a fee simple. You can do that by simply engaging or hiring a title company to search out who the party is or who the payments are going to, which is part of public record. There is a calculation that is equal to, depending upon which part of the country it is in, five to seven years' worth of payments on that lease. That ends up being your buyout amount. The leases are very inexpensive, typically less than $250 a year as a whole.

The pros and cons are that you buy out the lease and now have a fee-simple property, which is an all-inclusive title on both the land and the building or structure. That becomes a very useful tool in moving forward, especially if you're doing seller financing, because you can leverage that type of property better than you can leverage a lease hold property when you get into the big dollars.

The next type of title is a co-op, which is very common in New York, Philadelphia, Florida and DC. A co-op takes the concept of teamwork; in this case when you buy, for example, a condo, you don't technically buy or own the property. Instead, you buy shares in a corporation that owns the entire physical structure or building, and then the shares are what you own. You have X number of shares based on the amount of square footage or the overall value of the property and what you paid for it. It's like buying into a corporation.

Typically, each shareholder has an equal say as a whole in the co-op in how it is run and how it is maintained. A lot of people don't understand that because you are not really buying a fee simple title. You are buying a share in a corporation, which some investors, depending upon their knowledge, are okay with because they understand the structure of it, and some investors stay away from it because they don't understand the structure of it or it doesn't fit into their investing model as a whole. They may understand it completely, but it has a way of skewing their numbers, or if they are doing a hypothecation with their portfolios, it may be kicked out by the bank because the bank doesn't like those kinds of things. It really depends on what their end goal is and whether or not that enhances their portfolio because if it does, they will buy it. If it doesn't enhance their portfolio, then they won't buy it.

The next part when you get into properties is really paying attention, especially with properties that are in natural disaster areas or properties that have been rehabbed and put back on the market. One of the things you really want to pay attention to are non-permitted additions to the property. It's great to have more square footage. It raises the value of the property. It does all kinds of wonderful things. If you have additions to the property that bring more square footage that were not permitted, and they didn't go through the proper chain of title in getting the permits and getting the city's approval or the county's approval, then ultimately, you are going to potentially run into issues.

Not so much that you would be legally responsible for it as the lien holder, but if the homeowner is challenged with the legalities of it, the city comes along and says, "Wait a minute, this room addition was not permitted, and we don't show it on our records anywhere. It was just done under the radar." Now we want this thing permitted, but they are not going to go back to the prior owner. They are going to go back to the current owner, which happens to be your client. That client is now going to be burdened with a legal challenge with the city or county, and they are going to have to come out of pocket for legal costs, as well as having to invest time to figure out how to resolve the situation. That in itself can be a major deterrent and/or turnoff, and it could potentially send your home buyer running down the street, especially if they have very little down payment.

If they've only got 5% down on the house and that house is a $60,000 house, they put $3,000 down. Six months into moving into the house, all of a sudden they are getting a knock at the door from the city inspector saying, "Wait a minute, you have this addition on this house, and we don't show that ever being permitted. We need to talk." That homeowner will very quickly decide whether or not this is something they want to be involved in or if they are just going to quit paying on the mortgage because they think the mortgage company or you as the note holder is responsible for it, and they want you to handle it. If you don't do it, then they will just stop making mortgage payments on it, which ultimately leads to a foreclosure, which ultimately means that now you end up with the property back, and now you have to deal with it as the mortgage holder.

These types of changes to houses bring in extra square footage, extra value and they tend to be part of a bigger picture, a much more beautiful picture in regard to the overall quality of the property. However, what they also tend to do is bring the potential of risk to the lien holder. That's true whether or not you are buying seller finance papers or whether you are Bank of America lending on a house.

How do you discover that?

It is pretty easy to discover it because when you pull the tax records, the tax records show X square footage on the property. Usually tax records are slow to update. Then you do an appraisal on the property. They are going to measure the square footage of that property, and it needs to be equal on both sides. It can be off by a couple of square feet, which is not a big issue. If it is off by 300, or 400, or 500 square feet, something has happened. It doesn't necessarily mean that it was illegally done. You just need to go the extra step and find out if in fact there was a permit that was obtained.

Some additions can be done without permits. Those are different from city to city or county to county. Those you will just have to investigate on your own. Title companies can also research this for you. They have tremendous tools and resources available at their fingertips. They can also dig in and find out these types of things for you as well. You see this sometimes with pools. Here in Arizona, one of the things that can be an issue when you are buying a note on a property is if the house had a pool, and all of a sudden it no longer has a pool. That typically means that that person had that pool removed. Technically speaking, they have to file for a permit to do that. The truth is, very few of them ever do.

What they end up doing is they pull off the pool deck around the pool, they break the pool down about two feet below the waterline, and they just dump everything into the bottom of the pool and fill it up with dirt and cover it up. It sounds like a great idea until you go to do something in your backyard, or if you get a heavy rain, which we do occasionally a couple times a year, where it will settle that dirt in a way where all of a sudden you end up with a big sinkhole in your backyard. Not necessarily life or death, but certainly an eye opener for a new homeowner buying that property. It's things like these that you just need to make sure as a whole.

One of the things that we do when we are working with a client and building out a model seller finance division for the rehabber is to meet with them and find out the overall quality of work that they are doing. We will go through and inspect several houses and see if their tendency is to cut corners, or if their tendency is to go the extra mile and do the right thing for the property as a whole. These are some basic things that you really want to keep an eye out for.

Back in the 70's my grandparents converted their garage. Although they left the garage door on the garage, so it still looked like a garage from the exterior, they drywalled over the interior side of it, and they put carpet in it. They didn't structurally change anything, including the wiring or plumbing. They took the garage door opener off the ceiling and made it look like a room, and it could easily be converted back. That's not the type of stuff we're looking at. What we're looking at are things like pulling off the garage doors and putting windows up, adding a bathroom or kitchenette – structural things.

I know there's going to be some investors out there that are like, "Troy, you're making a mountain out a molehill." I would agree that that's probably true on a lot of what I would call light rehabs. What we are really looking for here is if they are changing the footprint of the house and is this a violation of the city code or are they environmental issues.

Here's a great example. We had a deal that we did in San Antonio, Texas. We went to purchase the note on the property, and the property looked like any other house. It was remodeled, it was cleaned up, people were living in it. From the street, it looked like any normal house. What we didn't realize, until we pulled title on it, was that there was a $36,000 tire lien on the house. Mind you, this is a brick and mortar house. This has nothing to do with tires, and it was not a modular home or a mobile home that got converted. It was brick and mortar, pier and beam house. There was a tire lien as in T-I-R-E, like car tires. The investor bought the house through a tax foreclosure, a tax deed. When he bought it, there were no tires. It was in a state of repairs, but there were no tires.

What we found out was a year and a half earlier the city had come in and taken truckloads of car tires and truck tires off the property because they were a potential fire hazard. The previous owner had used it as a makeshift tire shop and auto repair shop. We didn't have any EPA issues, meaning soil contamination, but we did have the tires lien and we had to actually go in and renegotiate with the city of San Antonio. We finally got them to agree to $3,700 to release the lien.

All I'm trying to stress here is that different things may affect the value. You can buy a property that has minor issues, but you want to go in with your eyes open in valuing the note with the assumption that you might have to solve these problems I have talked about.

The great part about being a note investor is that you can control the entire deal. You get to make the decisions on whether or not this is something you are okay with or whether or not it is something you want to pass on. Knowing that these things are out there, they will pop up the longer you are in the business and the more deals that you do. We may even tend to see remodels or additions to properties without permits as being a very big trend in our industry in the near future because what we are seeing even here in the Phoenix marketplace is that investors are going in, they're buying these older homes, typically three-bedroom, two bath homes and their changing the footprint.

For example, you have the main house, a carport, a walkthrough, and an exterior laundry room. Not many people want an exterior laundry room. They want that laundry room inside their house. What they are doing is enclosing that carport, making it into a garage and adding that square footage, and bringing that laundry room into the house, technically speaking. Although it's still all under one roof, it becomes livable square footage, which brings up their value. These remodels or additions are very inexpensive to do, typically less than $5,000 or $6,000, but they add tremendous value. A $5,000 remodel addition adds $15,000 value to the bottom line.

It never hurts to just put a call into the local building inspector and ask them if there are any problems he's aware of with your property and/or any of the other properties in the neighborhood.

The Power of Paper

Chapter 10

Performing Notes – Wholesaling vs Investor

In this chapter, I want to share with you the two different sides of the performing note business. The two sides can be easily summed up as the *wholesaling* side and the *investor* side. I'm going to first talk about the wholesaling side of the business because that's where I got my start at.

When I was first introduced to this industry, the one thing I didn't have was money. I was a single guy living in a two-bedroom town house. Although I had a good attorney friend of mine teach me the industry, that still didn't give me the money to invest in notes. As a matter of fact, what we focused on was wholesaling. Now the traditional definition of wholesaling, and it's used quite frequently in the brick and mortar side of the business, is the fix and flip side of the business. You go out and identify a property, get it under contract, sell it to an investor, and ultimately make a small margin of spread on the sale. Aka wholesaling the house.

Well the same thing happens in the paper business. Now I'm going to talk about it from a street level perspective, but there's also a Wall Street level perspective on it as well. The street Level perspective, which is something anybody can do in the market space, is to go out and identify notes. (Performing, first lien, and then you can do some second liens.) Then get them under contract. (We like to use an option agreement.) You can find copy of the option agreement in the resource guide. But in doing so, we use that to get the deal under contract.

Now, what does that mean? What does that entail? What are we looking for when we are wholesaling out a note? Well the number one thing we are looking for is obviously a willing seller. A willing seller is somebody who has sold a property. They have carried back the note and mortgage on the property and now they want to unlock their cash that's tied up in that documentation (meaning the note mortgage.) They want to typically unlock it because they want to go and buy another property. Or they have other investments that they would much rather put their money into. In other words, they are turning dollars on a regular basis. They can't turn dollars that are locked up.

So along comes a person like myself, or yourself. You identify that they've got a property that they have sold with a note on it and that they are motivated to sell. Once that's identified, we go through a series of checks and balances: we identify the type of note that it is (first or second), we identify the rates, the terms, the down payment, the property type, the borrower's credit, and we go through that checks and balance list. Once we go through that list, we now have an idea of what that seller has to offer or has for sell.

Now here's the most amazing part about this business. Unlike a lot of wholesaling models where you typically have to be in the local area to do this (meaning brick and mortar), in the note business, you can wholesale nationwide. I would say ninety-nine percent of the deals that we do are somewhere outside of the state of Arizona. We don't typically do a lot in the state of Arizona because Arizona tends to be one of the hotter spots for real estate in any given market. So there's not a lot of seller financing that takes place. With that being said, we are in turn able to do business nationwide.

The easiest way to outline the quality of deal that a seller is selling is to simply use our mortgage worksheet. Our mortgage worksheet is located in the resource site as well. What you are doing is basically taking that mortgage worksheet, filling it out completely, which will operate as a Q and A session between you and the seller, and it will provide you with all the information you need in order to effectively market that particular note.

Now in marketing that particular note, who would you sell it to? Well, you could sell it to a private investor; somebody who has an IRA and wants to buy it. You could sell it to banks; there are banks around the country that will buy notes. You can sell it to a friend or family member who is looking to park some money for long term residual income. You can also sell it to pension plans, insurance companies, to Wall street, foreign investors...the list goes on.

Now what do we mean by marketing the deal? Let's say you are an investor or a wholesaler and you find a house in Dallas, Texas. If that house has value, meaning you are able to buy it below market value, and you put it under contract, now you have to find somebody to buy it.

Most investors, or wholesalers, will have a Rolodex full of investors that they can easily call and in turn give that investor the opportunity to buy it and figure out what their margin is. Whether it's a couple thousand dollars or ten or twenty thousand dollars, it varies from deal to deal.

The same thing is true in the note business. When we wholesale a note, I can easily take that mortgage worksheet and I can send it over to buyer. Once they give me their pay price, I can easily go back to the seller and negotiate out my fee between connecting the two dots. Case in point - Say it was a $100,000 note. I could find a buyer that might pay eighty cents on the dollar. That eighty percent would be unpaid principal balance. I could in turn sell it back to, or negotiate with the seller to pay them seventy-five cents on the dollar, meaning there would be approximately a $5,000 fee in there for me to in turn connect the buyer and the seller together. Now using my option agreement, you could very easily put the deal under contract. For $75,000, you can assign that option agreement to the buyer who quoted you $80,000. And by doing so, when they close the deal, after due diligence, they will wire $75,000 to the seller and they will wire $5,000 to your checking or savings account. Wherever you instruct them to do it.

Now the beauty of this is that these deals typically will pay out in wholesale fees anywhere between 3-6%. Very similar to a real estate agent. We do tend to mirror a lot of supporting industries primarily because it's fair and it's reasonable and it's already a proven model. With that being said, you now have a template that can assure you, or outline for you what you can make on each deal. Meaning anywhere from 3-6% on every single deal that you do.

The beauty of wholesaling is that our note industry is approximately a one point seven-billion-dollar industry. Keeping in mind that 13-16% of all of residential real estate sold each year is done with seller financing.

Now every single month there are more and more notes that are being created, which means that there are more and more opportunities for you to succeed as a wholesaler. The best part about being a wholesaler is that you don't need a lot of tools and resources to succeed. Some basic things that you would need would be a computer, a phone, a fax machine, or a way to fax. You want to have some basic software on your computer like Microsoft Windows, which is very common today. You also want to have a basic website and some business cards. With that, you're essentially a wholesaler for all intents and purposes. You don't have to have large lines of credit; you just have to have a little bit of money in order to set up your website and do some basic things.

But with that, it gives you the power and ability to do business on a nationwide basis. Through having that ability to do business nationwide, you are able to focus and hone in on the motivated sellers of real estate notes.

The Power of Paper

Why do I say that? Well, because it's not every day that everybody's interested in selling their notes. Let's just be honest. That's just a fact. But that's no different than the brick and mortar side of the business because not every day are people interested in selling their house.

With that being said, let's compare you to a brick and mortar investor... A brick and mortar investor is somewhat limited on the area that they can cover. Meaning, if they are here in Phoenix, they have to work the Phoenix marketplace. Whereas as a note investor doesn't have to work the Phoenix marketplace. I do on occasion, but I work nationwide based on the motivated sellers that are ready to sell today. I don't tend to worry about the other people that aren't ready to sell.

Now why is that? Because when people are ready to sell, by having a website on the internet, they will find you. That requires some SEO, and some marketing, and things like that. But by doing that, you open yourself up to a much larger base of sellers than you would if you were just focusing on a particular city or zip code. This is very common with brick and mortar investors.

Now the beauty of wholesaling is that number one, you can do it nationwide. Number two, it's a very low barrier to entry, meaning it doesn't cost a lot of money to get started. Number three, you have no capital at risk. Number four, you get to earn and learn at the same time. You're out there, you're learning the business, you're learning the ropes. You are learning what it takes to do due diligence. You are learning what it takes to market. You are learning the paper work. You are learning how to get evaluations. How to retitle commitment and policies. You are learning all of those things and at the same time you're learning it and earning at the same time.

In other words, when you go through the wholesaling process, and you sign that contract over, you do not have to do the due diligence on the file. That is not a responsibility of the wholesaler. Now I do highly recommend that as a wholesaler you do some basic due diligence. The more you can HELP buyers gather the paper work that they need, the faster your deal comes together. But that's more of a matter of investing some time over investing your dime.

The beauty of wholesaling is it doesn't cost money to wholesale notes. It cost you, and takes, a little bit of time. But through that, you gain the education, you gain the relationship, and you build your book of business, all inclusive of one another.

Investor Side

If you are an investor in the business and buying performing notes, there are two reasons people purchase notes. The first reason is they buy them with the intention of keeping them for long term residual value. They are putting whatever capital they have out and are looking at enjoying the monthly or quarterly payments that come in from that. Second, they like the return it provides them. Now the return is going to vary from note to note for a lot of different reasons. But I will come back to that in a little bit. The point here is that people have different motivations in what they want and what they plan to do with their money.

Whereas you or I may think, "Well, I'm not going to invest any note unless it produces me an 18% return." Okay. Well that is definitely an option. But I'll be the first to tell you to buy a performing note on 18% return, or yield. I can tell you from experience that this means that you're not going to be buying a lot of deals.

Whereas an investor that's buying, say, at a 10 or 11% percent yield is going to buy more deals than you or me. Now people often ask, "What is an investor's yield?" Well, I'll simply share this with you. Investor's yield is determined by the overall cost of their capital. So, if an investor has money sitting in a trust fund or they have money sitting in a savings account or a mutual fund account, or maybe they just sold their business and they want to invest, that money has a tendency to what we refer to in the business as a zero cost of capital.

It's not costing them anything for it to sit there. But it's also not making them any money with it sitting there. And they know that; and we know that. The point is if somebody has a zero cost of capital, if they go out and start looking for notes, and they are willing to accept an 8, 9 or 10% yield, that means that they are going to pay more for that note than what you or I would if we were trying to get a 15 or 18% yield. Now I'm not saying that's what we do. I'm just using this as an overall example.

The point is that when an investor is out buying, he or she will set their own rates of return based on what they see as the overall goal for their capital. So, if their goal is to get a 10% return, and they've got zero cost of capital, then it's really easy to set their money at a 10% yield.

If you're an investor and you've borrowed money from a line of credit at the bank, then that borrowed money is going to come with a cost - three, four or five percent. So, if you are trying to get a premium on that, meaning ten percent over that, then you are going to be buying stuff at a 15% yield.

Now I share that with you to go back to a moment ago, where I said there's two things to do in this business. You can either wholesale, which is your "earn and learn" model. It doesn't cost you capital. And you don't put capital at risk. But you also don't earn the residual returns that an investor who's investing money would earn.

Now there's a basic rule of thumb here. You have to keep this in mind when you're in the marketplace. Performing notes are typically being purchased in today's marketplace anywhere between 7 to 14% yield. Now the difference between the two, or the difference in that spread is 1. Capital and 2. Risk.

Now what would risk look like in an investment of this nature? Well risk might look like a low-down payment from the borrower. It might look like poor credit. It might look like very little seasoning. Definitely some seasoning is very few payments having been made on the loan. It also might be looked at as an area, like a zip code or a county. Something along those lines. Typically, it's done by zip code. But an area that has what were referred to as war zone areas. Rough neighborhoods. Every city has them throughout the country. That would be a risk factor. The condition of the property would be a risk factor. Is this property in good condition? Does it have good curb appeal? Things of that nature might be a risk factor.

Rural areas can be a risk factor. Now some people may say, "Well that's not a risk factor. It's on the outskirts, in farm country." Understandable, but keep in mind that when you buy rural properties, those types of properties will sometimes come with the risk of, "if you do have to take them back, how fast can I resell it at the end of the day?"

Another risk factor might be the interest rate that the seller used to originate the loan. If they are using a low interest rate, in comparison to Bank of America or Wells Fargo, then that's going to affect their purchase price or what they would receive for that note.

So, if you or I lend money on a note at a 3% interest rate, because the institutions are doing this, and we find a buyer that's wanting to buy at a 10% yield, on a thirty-year term, that is going to be a huge discount to the pay price of that note. It is a simple mathematical equation. The longer the money is out there, and the smaller the interest rate, the bigger the discount. That's the simplicity behind it.

So those are some basic aspects of the risk. Now, every investor that buys notes looks at it from that perspective. The number one thing that they hate as an investor is the idea of taking back the home through a foreclosure. Now why do I say that? Well, because there is another side to our industry, and that's called a Non-Performing Loan side, or an NPL side. The NPL side is a different model altogether. It's like apple and oranges.

The NPL side, because it's a different model, works off of different calculations and different returns. But it also works off of more heavy lifting. Whereas the performing notes side, which I was just sharing with you, deals with more of a plug and play type investment. Meaning, if you bring me a note, I purchase it and agree to buy it from you as a wholesaler (let's say I was back to my original example of $80,000) I'm going to pay you $80,000, and you negotiated with the seller that you would buy it for $75,000 and you get to keep the five thousand. That's not a problem. That is very commonplace in our business.

So as an investor who's invested capital and looking for a greater return of 10%, the one thing I don't want to get involved with is buying a note that's performing. That's a plug and play investment from you. In other words, I'm going to deploy my capital. I'm going to park the note with a servicing company. I'm going to allow the servicing company to maintain it for me. But because it's a performing note, if it goes into default, now I run the risk of being literally upside down in that matter. If I have to go and foreclose on that property, there are a couple of key elements that you have to realize as an investor that come into play:

1. I stop losing my return on my capital. So that operates as a negative.
2. I have to hire an attorney, or a trustee to handle the foreclosure. That's going to result in thousands of dollars for that to happen.

3. I now have to do what is called forced placed insurance on that property, to make sure that my house is protected.
4. I now have to keep up on the property taxes, so I don't lose the property to a tax sale.

Now, some people say, "It's not going to take that long to foreclose. Why would you do that?" Well, you want to make sure that everything stays in good standing with third party aspects like insurance companies, the county tax assessor's office and the HOA. You want to make sure that those accounts remain in good standing so that there are less issues down the road.

When you don't pay your county taxes, that accrues interest. You don't pay your insurance on the property, and the house gets vandalized or burned down, now all of a sudden, you are losing money because you have to remodel. You don't pay the HOA fees, those will accumulate with penalties and interest, to the point where the HOA could potentially foreclose on the property and knock you out of position. So all of those become extra work if you don't maintain those expenses. By maintaining those expenses, that means more money out of my pocket to recover my investment at the end of the day.

This is the way an investor thinks when he or she is looking at a deal on the front side. What is the potential of losing this property? What is the potential of this property going into foreclosure? If it does that, I will accrue interest, I will have to pay taxes, insurance, HOA fees, legal fees, recording fees, prep fees...all of those things in order to recover my investment back.

So, being a $100,000 note on a $110,000 sales price and paying $80,000, I could very easily eat up a good $10,000 over a six-month period to foreclose on that property. The average length of time to foreclose on property on a nationwide basis is like 6.3 months. In doing so, that could eat up an easy ten grand. Now I could also add on a few more things: once I get the property back, now I have to clean it up, maintain it, sell it. I'm also going to need to find a realtor to list it for me. That realtor's going to want 4-6%. They get 3%, the buyer gets 3%. Why do you do that? Because that attracts buyer's agents, and it gets your agent to work hard for you because it pays more.

That's just logical. Actually, it is a little inside secret! The point is you're going to pay 6%. So, if you were able to sell it for a $100,000, that's $6,000. If you spent $10,000 in legal costs and holding time, taxes and insurance, now you have another $6,000 on top of that. You are back to recovering your investment and making about $3,000 or $4,000 over a 6-9-month time period.

With that said, those are the kinds of realities that come with the note investing marketplace. So, what determines whether a house is going to go into foreclosure or not on the beginning side? As an investor, there are a couple of key elements that we pay close attention to: 1. Is it affordable? Meaning, what is the individual making? What can they truly afford versus what their income is? Is the property affordable? If somebody's only making $2,000 a month, but their mortgage payment is $1,000 a month, that's going to result in a default sooner versus later.

2. Did they put money down? Ideally 10% down would be great. That would be ideal. 10% or more would be even better. What's the borrower's credit like? Is it north of 625? Is it south of 625? If it's south of 625, the reality of it is that you are going to see a higher number of defaults with performing mortgages with people that have lower credit than with people that have higher credit.

That applies to all of us across this country. Whether we are able to borrow money from banks or not, the lower our credit score is, that is an indicator to creditors that we are a potential credit risk. That's a governing factor. That is something that we do look at as investors. Why do we look at it? It's not that we look at it because we are an institutional investor. We look at it because we don't want to lose money. For that matter, we don't want anybody to lose money.

More importantly, *we don't want to lose money.*

As an investor, when we are looking at a deal that first comes to us and we are reviewing their credit, one of the things that we are looking for on their credit is the age of the accounts. Meaning that if they have a low credit score and they have a whole bunch of recent charge offs in the last 6-12 months, that's an indicator of the season that person's currently in in their life.

But the other side is true, where we have seen low credit scores, and we look at the collection account, or accounts with issues, and we see that they are from two or three years ago, but they are back on their feet. They have a solid job, solid income, but they just haven't had a chance to rebuild their credit, even though they have a substantial down payment. That to me is a better investment than somebody that has a bigger down payment, but lower credit, and all the issues are very recent.

Case in point: I remember a deal that came to me in Phoenix. It was a beautiful house. It was a half a million-dollar deal. And we pulled the gentleman's credit. Although the gentleman's credit was a 690, we passed on the deal because in the recent years he had a car repossessed, he had two houses foreclosed on, and he had been through a bankruptcy.

What that told us as an investor is that this person has had challenges. But he has now learned the ropes in how he can work against us as an investor. So, if he runs into financial difficulties again, what is he going to do? He's going to drag us through the mud with these types of tools and resources, which he is legally entitled to do. But we don't want to be part of it.

In other words, it gets back to prior to buying the note, you have options and choices, so you are going to make the best ones you can.

You know, buying a note is no different than buying a house from the investor's side. We are looking at that deal to identify the risk and the reward. And we are looking at it with the intention of holding it long term. Now we mainly hold it on a short-term basis, meaning, if we buy that at ten yield and six months later we sell it to somebody else at an eight yield, we make a couple points. But that's a plan C in regard to being an investor.

Sometimes investors will do that because it replenishes their capital. It obviously gives them a return as well. And sometimes the deal just needs little more seasoning. You know, being a note buyer, we buy after one month of seasoning. So we buy something at one month, and we season it for, say, six to twelve months. We can sell that off in a package of notes and get a higher pay price on that package down the road. So those are some tricks that we use similar to people in the brick and mortar side of the business as well.

The Power of Paper

Conclusion

In conclusion, investing in mortgage notes can be a profitable, lucrative and rewarding business venture. Think about it like this...Mapmakers once drew dragons on maps to warn sailors of the risk involved with entering unexplored waters. After seeing these drawings, some sailors literally believed that a dragon inhabited the ocean. These sailors refused to venture beyond safe, known territory.

Other sailors saw the dragon differently. They recognized that the dragon symbolized adventure, an opportunity to learn and grow and see new things.

Like the sailors, you're entering foreign territory when you invest in mortgages. You can view this form of investing as something to be feared and avoided or you can recognize it as a new opportunity.

The choice is yours!

If you are ready to either take your Note Business to the next level or start your very own Note Investing Business, then register to get our FREE course, *Mortgage Investor Pro*. It will give you all the resources and training you need to build and monetize your Note Business:

www.mortgageinvestorpro.com/resource/

If you want to learn more about my company or to submit a request for pricing on your note, check out our site at:

www.pinnacle-investments.com

We also have several other educational trainings that you can check out. They, too, will help jumpstart your business...

The Power of Paper

Power of Paper: This training educates students on finding and flipping residential notes. In it I will teach you how to buy, hold and flip to Institutional Buyers for maximum profits. This is an online home study training.

In this training I cover:
- What Banks are Buying
- Autopilot Marketing
- Where's the Money in the Deal
- Smart Contract and How It Works
- 10 Day Closings and How They Work

http://tipoplive.com/

US NPL Summit: In this training I show students how to tap into the HUGE market of SFR Non-Performing Notes on a nationwide basis. The current size of the SFR NPN market is estimated at $570 Billion. This is an online home study training.

In this training I cover:
- Note Default Risk Assessment / Underwriting Criteria
- Servicing – Due Diligence, On-Boarding Communication and & Monitoring
- Compliance Issues Surrounding Buying and Servicing NPL's
- Banks & Mortgage Originators Working out NPL's
- Acquisition, Due Diligence and Collateral Evaluation
- Raising, Managing and Projecting Capital Cost for your Portfolio
- And Much More…

www.usnplsummit.com

Commercial Note Pro: In this training I show students how to buy, sell and wholesale Commercial notes. This is an online home study training.

In this training I cover:
- How to Market and Find Commercial Properties
- How to Find, Identify and Work Commercial Real Estate Deals Nationwide
- How to Find and Wholesale Commercial Notes
- How to Find and Purchase NPL's from Banks (at discounts)
- How to Work with Capital Groups to Fund Your Deals
- And Much More

www.commercialnotepro.com

ABC's of Simo's: In this training I cover Simultaneous Closings and how they work. If you want to double your note wholesaling and buying business, then you have to understand how to structure deals that increase the seller profit and protect the investor at the same time. This is an online home study training.

In this training I cover:
- What a Simultaneous Closing is
- How to use Simultaneous Closings to Sell and Wholesale Properties
- How to use Simultaneous Closings to Buy Real Estate (both Residential and Commercial)
- How to use an LLC so That You Can Control the Properties and Protect Yourself

www.abcofsimos.com

The Power of Paper

Free Investor Resources

Get the tools and educational resources you need to start your own Mortgage Investing Business.

Go here to get all of your tools and 50+ videos to guide your journey to success:

www.mortgageinvestorpro.com/resource/

Sign Up Today

The Power of Paper

About the Author

Troy Fullwood is a skilled investment professional with over 22 years of experience in the industry. A graduate of Arizona State University, Troy founded Pinnacle Investments in 1996. Under his expert guidance, Pinnacle Investments has grown to be the nation's leader in the purchase of first lien performing and non-performing real estate notes, completing over 15,000 transactions since its inception. The professionals at Pinnacle Investments set the standard for high quality, strategic growth and pride themselves on their unique ability to help struggling individuals keep their homes.

In 2007, Troy built Wall Street's first distressed asset fund, which he ran for two years before selling his interest to a Wall Street Capital group. During his tenure, the fund earned a strong internal rate of return and helped thousands of people stay in their homes due to loan restructuring under Troy's guidance.

Troy is recognized as one of the industry's top investment professionals and is often asked to speak at financial conferences and companies such as American Cashflow, Investor Wealth, and Peak Potentials. He also contributes his ideas on real estate investing through numerous published articles and radio talk show interviews. Troy has received multiple awards throughout his career including being voted the 2015 Best Mortgage Investor USA by Wealth & Finance International and Best of the Best in Finance by Acquisition International in 2016. When not working, Troy is active in his church and assists his community with financial issues.

Recent Career Highlights:

1996: Founder of Pinnacle Investments – A nationwide buyer of notes with over 15,000 closed note transactions

2015: Best Mortgage Investor USA by Wealth & Finance International

2016 – 2017: Best of the Best in Finance by Acquisition International

2017: Member of the Seller Finance Coalition based in Washington DC.

2017: Led legislative meetings on Capitol Hill as a Supporter of Bill H.R. 1360

2017: Bestselling International author of Thought Leaders of Business Expert Forum at Harvard

2017: Launched "The Thriving Investor" Financial Website

2017: Spoke at Harvard Business School

2017: Spoke at NASDEQ

Troy@pinnacle-investments.com

www.pinnacle-investments.com

480-831-5067

The Power of Paper

Made in the USA
Coppell, TX
20 February 2021